History of Lochleven Castle: With Details of the Imprisonment and Escape of Mary Queen of Scots

Robert Burns-Begg, Begg (Robert Burns-)

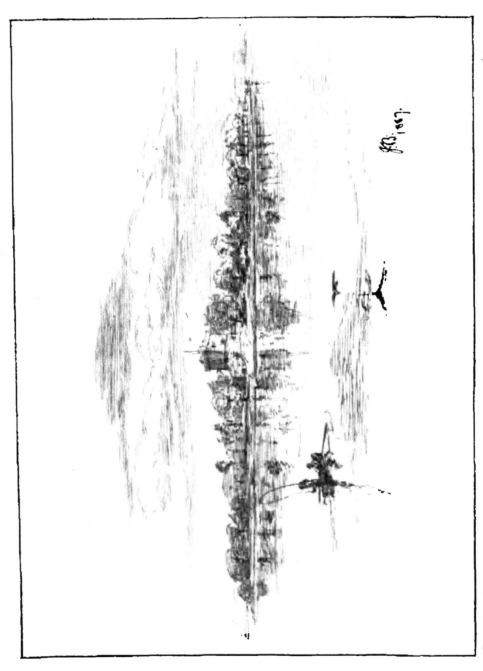

Frontispiece.

THE CASTLE ISLAND.
(from the north east)

HISTORY
OF
LOCHLEVEN CASTLE

WITH DETAILS OF

THE IMPRISONMENT AND ESCAPE OF
MARY QUEEN OF SCOTS

"Shipwrecked on a kingdom."
SHAKSPERE.

BY ROBERT BURNS-BEGG, F.S.A. Scot.
AUTHOR OF "THE LOCHLEVEN ANGLER"

ILLUSTRATED BY JOHN BEGG

SECOND EDITION.

KINROSS: GEORGE BARNET
MDCCCLXXXVII.

TO

SIR GRAHAM GRAHAM MONTGOMERY

OF STANHOPE, BARONET

THE PRESENT "LAIRD OF LOCHLEVEN"

This Volume is Dedicated

AS A

TRIBUTE OF RESPECT AND GRATITUDE

ILLUSTRATIONS.

CONTENTS.

CHAPTER I.

INTRODUCTORY.

CHAPTER II.

EARLY HISTORY OF THE CASTLE.

CHAPTER III.

QUEEN MARY AT LOCHLEVEN CASTLE.

CHAPTER IV.

QUEEN MARY'S IMPRISONMENT.

CHAPTER V.

QUEEN MARY'S IMPRISONMENT—*continued.*

CHAPTER VI.

QUEEN MARY'S ESCAPE.

CONCLUSION.

APPENDICES.

PREFACE.

THE following pages consist simply of a reproduction, in a much more extended form, of a Lecture which the Author, as Honorary President of the Glasgow Kinross-shire Association, had the privilege of delivering to that Association in Glasgow last year. The work is of an unpretentious character, and is merely an attempt to relate in plain and simple language, and in a properly consecutive and intelligible form, the various historic incidents which have from time to time occurred within and around Lochleven Castle, and more particularly those deeply interesting associations which connect it with the sad but interesting life of Mary Queen of Scots. As the Prison in which she passed the first year of her life-long captivity, and as the scene of her romantic escape temporarily from the hands of her enemies, the Castle can never fail to be an object of attraction and interest, not to the natives of Kinross-shire only, but to Scotsmen generally, and to this interesting portion of the narrative special attention has been devoted with the view of making it as minute as a due regard to historical authenticity permits.

When we consider the mass of literature which the wide-spread interest in Queen Mary has called into existence, and the fullness with which the details of her brief life are therein investigated and treated of, it may seem alike bold and pre-sumptuous thus to hazard an additional tiny contribution, but of all the incidents in the life of the unhappy Queen, her prison experiences within Lochleven Castle formed the one episode of which, until within the last three years, little or nothing was really known. Her life as the Queen Consort of France, her public career as Queen of Scotland, and her prison life in England, have all been narrated in elaborate detail; but the first long weary year of her experience as a State Prisoner had remained enveloped in all but total obscurity, until the veil was partially drawn aside by the recent publication of Nau's "Memoir."

That contemporary document, which for the last three centuries has lain unread among the Cottonian MSS., is in the hand-writing of Claud Nau, a Frenchman of family and position, who officiated as Queen Mary's private secretary for nearly twelve years during her captivity in England; and the information on which its narrative is based was clearly derived from the illustrous captive herself, as well as from those members of her retinue who shared her imprisonment in Lochleven Castle and aided her in her escape. That "Memoir" supplies many of the details not hitherto known to history which are introduced into the following pages; and it was mainly from a desire to bring these additional details under the notice of the Glasgow Kinross-shire Association that the Author was induced to select "Queen Mary's Imprisonment and Escape" as the subject of his recent lecture.

Nau's "Memoir," as edited by the Rev. Mr Stevenson, is unfortunately not put before the public in a form adapted for popular perusal, and it is therefore little likely to awaken the public interest which it is well calculated to secure. Written in the French language of three centuries ago, and composed by one who was entirely dependent on others for information as to the incidents he is narrating, and the scenes in which these occurred, the "Memoir" is of a somewhat fragmentary character, and often obscure and confused in its phraseology, and it is only by a careful study of its terms, and a more or less general re-arrangement of its order and sequence, that the real import and true meaning of the narrative can be arrived at. Alike in the original French, and in Mr Stevenson's careful translation of it, the "Memoir" has been subjected to this ordeal, and its reliability has been further tested by care-fully verifying within the ruins themselves many of its local details, and the incidents as here narrated are strictly in accord-ance with a fair and legitimate construction of Nau's statement, when read in the light of the authentic history of the period. Nau's literal statements have, as far as possible, been rigidly

and conscientiously adhered to—in many instances his own
exact terms being adopted—and in no instance has anything
been super-added which was not either directly or by the clearest
possible implication entitled to be assumed as genuine and
undoubted fact.

Along with Nau's "Memoir" there has been carefully
studied another contemporary document by an anonymous
author, composed in Latin, and written in the year of Queen
Mary's escape, 1568. The original of this document is now
in the Vatican at Rome, and in all its more prominent incidents it is thoroughly corroborative of Nau's "Memoir," and
in some minor points it amplifies and renders more specific
the details which Nau supplies.

The design of the following work has been simply to throw
all the additional light possible on Queen Mary's associations
with the County of Kinross; and the other deeply interesting
events of her short reign are therefore referred to in the briefest
possible terms, and only in so far as such reference appeared
to be absolutely necessary in order to render more clear and
intelligible the local incidents falling to be treated of in these
pages. It would have been quite beyond the purpose contemplated, to enlarge on Queen Mary's career generally, or to
deal with events which have been already fully and ably treated
of in our historic literature.

With these prefatory observations this little work is left

to speak for itself, in the earnest hope that to those who are connected with Kinross-shire by ties of birth or otherwise, the perusal of the historic details which are here so imperfectly strung together, may tend to deepen the historic interest which inseparably attaches itself to that County.

HISTORY OF LOCHLEVEN CASTLE.

CHAPTER I.

INTRODUCTORY.

> "Ah ! what a warning for a thoughtless man ;
>   Could field or grove, could any spot of earth
>   Show to his eye an image of the pangs
>   Which it hath witnessed ; render back an echo
>   Of the sad steps by which it hath been trod."
>
> WORDSWORTH.

THE History of Lochleven Castle may be regarded as really forming the early History of the little County—Kinross-shire—in which its ruined pile still occupies so prominent and central a position.   Forming, as the strong-hold did for many centuries, the baronial residence of the feudal superior of the greater portion of that county, it may readily be supposed that no question of importance could arise within the limits of the district which did not ultimately fall under the arbitrament of "*the* Castle," and that every vicissitude which befell "*the* Castle," would sooner or later make itself felt within every homestead, however humble, situated within the radius of the baronial influence.

Kinross-shire is in point of population the smallest of all the Scotch counties, and, with the single exception of its sister county, Clackmannan, it is the smallest in point of superficial extent as well.   It occupies the eastern half of the long level strath which extends from Benarty and the Cleish Hills on the

A

south to the Ochil range on the north, and from the Lomond Hill on the east to the western extremity of the Ochils on the west. Its superficial area does not exceed 50,000 acres, or 75 square miles, and it contains only five Parishes—Kinross, Orwell, Portmoak, Tulliebole (now part of Fossoway), and Cleish, with small portions of the Parishes of Arngask, Forgandenny, and Dunfermline. It was disjoined from Fifeshire and erected into a separate county in the year 1426, and was placed under the heritable jurisdiction of "the Lairds of Lochleven," with right to use the privilege (?) of "pit and gallows,"—a right which they had apparently exercised unsparingly, if the skeletons unearthed half a century ago, at the old "Gallows Knowe," are competent witnesses. The county has always been rural in its general character, the only towns within its limits being the county town of Kinross, in the parish of the same name, which also forms the Burgh of the Barony of Kinross; and the town of Milnathort, in the parish of Orwell, situated about a mile to the north of the county town. Neither of these towns exceeds 2000 in population, while in the other parishes there are merely the small villages of Kinnesswood, Scotlandwell, Balgedie, and Cleish. In these towns and villages a limited trade in the manufacture of woollen and linen fabrics and other industrial enterprises, has from a very remote period been prosecuted, but never to an extent calculated to affect the original character of the county as generally agricultural, and dependant in the main on agricultural enterprise for its prosperity and vitality.

Small and unimportant as Kinross-shire is, there are few districts in the Lowlands of Scotland which present to the eye a more attractive picture of pleasing pastoral beauty and interest. The scenery is undoubtedly tame as compared with the more imposing grandeur of the Highlands of Perthshire and Stirlingshire; but in the verdure of its hills, the far spreading richness of its grassy plains, the luxuriance of its woods, and, more than aught else, in the wide expanse of the gleaming waters of Lochleven, with the sturdy but picturesque ruin of Lochleven Castle nestling in their very centre, the whole surroundings exhale an atmosphere of quiet, yet varied, beauty and placid repose. Of the scene, no truer or more artistic picture could be presented than that portrayed by Michael Bruce the Kinross-shire Poet, in his classic poem, "On Lochleven"—

> ". . . . . . . From the mountain's top
> Around me spread, I see the goodly scene,—
> Inclosures green, that promise to the swain
> The future harvest; many coloured meads;
> Irriguous vales, where cattle low, and sheep
> That whiten half the hills; sweet rural farms,
> Oft interspersed, the seats of pastoral love
> And innocence—with many a spiry dome
> Sacred to Heav'n, around whose hallow'd walls,
> Our fathers slumber in the narrow house.
> Gay beauteous villas bosomed in the woods
> Like constellations in the starry sky
> Complete the scene. The vales, the vocal hills,
> The woods, the waters, and the heart of man
> Send out a general song; 'tis beauty all
> To poet's eye, and music to his ear."

In its historical associations too, the county possesses attractions of more than ordinary importance. It is true that in point of national interest, and as the scene of important events in our national history, it can never vie with Stirlingshire, where, on the field of Bannockburn the final blow was struck against English domination; but, within its narrow limits, historic scenes have been enacted, and historic events have occurred, which appeal to the public interest and sympathy as powerfully and as irresistibly as do the more patriotic struggles recorded in Scottish history.

The few relics of pre-historic times which Kinross-shire possesses, are unfortunately neither very exceptional nor important in their character. They consist merely of an interesting ancient canoe, which is still to be seen in the entrance hall of Kinross House, and which was found embedded in Lochleven, near to the Castle Island, after the lowering of the surface of the lake by the extensive drainage operations of upwards of sixty years ago; two gigantic upright stones in a field on Orwell Farm, near to the northern shore of Lochleven, popularly supposed to mark the site of an ancient Druidical place of worship; an interesting underground structure, partially laid bare within the last few years on the lands of Coldrain; and several cinerary urns, unmistakable relics of Pagan times, which have within the past half century been unearthed at Craigton, Shanwell, and Gellybank, and which are now deposited in the Antiquarian Museum in Edinburgh. These interesting relics of ages long gone by, discovered as they have been in widely different localities, embracing the whole, or nearly the whole of the level strath of which Kinross-shire consists, clearly indicate that from the most remote antiquity the district throughout was a populated one, and was not, like many of the larger and more important counties of Scotland, a mere trackless waste, abandoned as a fit haunt only for the wild ox, the wolf, and the bear; and it may certainly be concluded that, even in those remote days, civilisation as it then existed in Scotland, was not altogether awanting in Kinross-shire.

Leaving, however, these dim and nebulous ages, and glancing at less remote times, we find that at the time the Romans invaded Scotland (A.D. 80–85) Kinross-shire was, along with the stretch of country lying between the rivers Forth and Tay, stubbornly held and defended by the ancient Caledonians or

Picts, and that it formed the bulwark which successfully resisted the attempt made by the Romans in Agricola's sixth campaign to force their way northwards along the east coast of Fife. The Romans, in their repeated efforts to extend their conquest beyond the Forth, penetrated into Fife as far as Lochore, lying within three miles of the southern shore of Lochleven, and separated from it by the intervening hill of Benarty. At Lochore they established a strongly fortified camp, which was intended to form their base for further and more extended incursions into the district held so tenaciously by the Picts. In this encampment one of the divisions of the Roman army, consisting of the 9th Legion, is understood to have passed the winter of 83-4; and in connection with the encampment, a military outwork or fortified point of observation is stated to have been established on the heights of Benarty. Beyond this point no traces of the Roman invaders have been found within the limits of Kinross-shire; and in their progress northwards during the following year they, instead of persisting in their original intention, adopted a more central route by marching round the south side of Benarty, and along the western limit of Kinross-shire by Fossoway and Glendevon. In all probability the ancient strong-holds of Cairnyvean, on the lands of Craigow on the Ochil Hills, and of Dumglow, on the Cleish Hills, belong to this period. Of these hill forts nothing now remains save shapeless piles of grey weather-beaten stones overgrown with moss and turf, and yet to the experienced eye they do not fail to tell of ramparts and battlements suited to the mode of warfare of the period.

From the date of the abandonment of the Roman occupation of the northern portion of Scotland down to the establishment of Christianity, about the middle of the sixth century, a thick impenetrable veil shrouds the history of Scotland, and its historians find little beyond mere probability and conjecture to guide them in their efforts to ascertain the character and circumstances of the different districts of the country during the intervening centuries. The absence of historical records is easily accounted for, both by the lack of education, and by the devotion to warlike pursuits and exercises which characterised these rude and troublous times   As Christianity, however, with its benign influence, strengthened its hold upon the country, a more peaceful and enlightened era began to dawn, and in a fragmentary way, clearer and more definite information is gleaned as to the local events of the period, and the character and habits of the people. Scotland, in this respect, is much indebted to its early Ecclesiastics, many of whom devoted themselves to the compilation of historical records of the public events of their day ; and among these early historians there is no one to whom Scotland owes more, or whose conscientious accuracy is more trustworthy than Andrew Winton, the ancient chronicler of Scotland, who, until 1420, officiated as Prior of a Monastery situated on an Island in Lochleven, lying about two miles to the south-west of the Island on which the ruins of Lochleven Castle now stand.

This ancient and important Ecclesiastical structure—the Priory of St Serf's—forms the subject of the earliest historical reference to the County of Kinross. It was founded in the later years of the eighth century by Brude V., the last King of the Picts, for the benefit of the Culdees, then established on the Island of St Serf's. This Culdee establishment is believed to stand next in priority in Scotland to that founded by St Columba in Iona in the year 562, and it continued to flourish vigorously for 400 years, when it was merged in the Priory of St Andrews. Even as late as the fifteenth century it continued

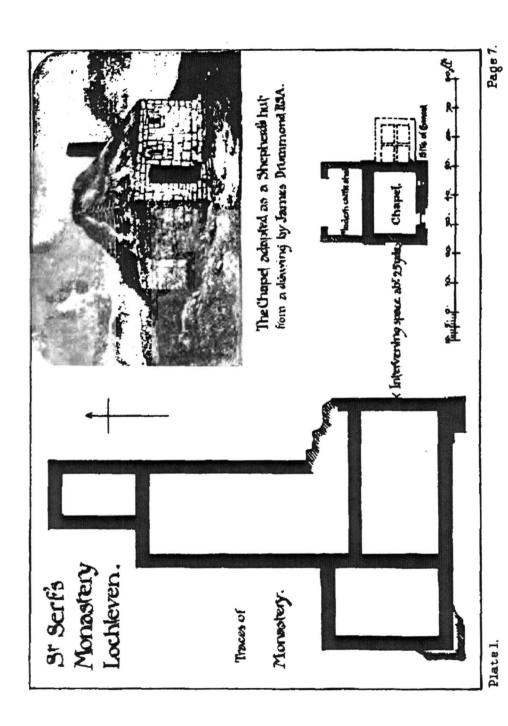

St Serf's
Monastery
Lochleven.

Traces of
Monastery.

The Chapel adapted as a Shepherd's hut
from a drawing by James Drummond R.S.A.

Modern cattle shed.

Chapel.

Site of Convent.

Interving space abt 25 yds.

Plate 1.   ECCLESIASTICAL REMAINS ON St SERF'S ISLAND   Page 7.

to rank as a Priory, and it was within its walls that Wyntoun penned his valuable "Cronykil of Scotland" in the earlier years of that century. The Priory was named after St Servanus, and it seems to have occupied for centuries a prominent place among the religious institutions of the period. It was liberally fostered and endowed by many of the regal successors of the original founder; for we find that Macbeth endowed it with the Lands of Kirkness and a portion of Bolguy; Malcolm III. with the Lands of Balchristie; and that King Edgar and other succeeding monarchs all made it the recipient of their pious benefactions.

Of the ruins of the Priory nothing now remains but a small portion of the walls of the Chapel, and the mere foundations of the adjoining Monastery, but these are still sufficient to indicate the original character and importance of the structure. A careful survey of the ruins was made five years ago by Mr Andrew Kerr, F.S.A. Scot., at the request of the Society of Antiquaries of Scotland, and the accompanying ground plan of the ruins (Pl. I.), and the following architectural details, are extracted from Mr Kerr's interesting report, which forms part of the published transactions of the society for the year 1881-2.

"The style of the masonry, and the impost mouldings of the west arch, show that it has been a plain building of the early Romanesque or Norman period—probably the eleventh century—and may be one of those churches stated to have been erected between 1040 and 1093. The outside dimensions of the chancel are 13 feet 6 inches long by 9 feet wide, and the foundation course of it was found to be divided longitudinally and across by thin stone walls, into four graves, in which were found nine complete human skeletons. The nave is 21 feet 6 inches long, and 14 feet 6 inches wide inside; what remains of walls are only 9 feet high ; semi-circular arches now built up appear at each end, the eastern one giving access to the chancel, and the other at the west end opening into a porch, or other apartment now taken down. Diggings have been made, but they disclose no foundations or trace of building ; the square window on the south is not original, as the lines of a circular headed window can be traced upon the inside face of the wall. The niche beside the door, and the holy water stoop inside appear also to be of a later period.

"About twenty-five yards west from the chapel the ground has been carefully opened, showing the extent of the remaining foundations of the old walls, and the tracks of the others which enabled the accompanying block plan of the monastic buildings to be prepared. Some details were also exposed which indicate that they may belong to about the fourteenth century, but from their irregular form it is probable that the whole may not have been erected at the same time."

"The plan now exhibited represents an area of about 650 superficial yards, exclusive of the chapel, which is sufficient to provide accommodation to the extent indicated by the ancient documents relating to the monastery. The two burying grounds required also by ancient rule, are provided here, the one upon St Serf's Island, and the other on the mainland at Portmoak."

Beyond the fact already referred to, that Wyntoun wrote his interesting and reliable "Cronykil of Scotland," in St Serf's Priory, no special event of public importance seems to have taken place on the Island. No doubt, from the isolated position of the Priory, and the clerical character and peaceful occupation of its inhabitants, life there would flow on from century to century in a placid monotonous stream, with little to disturb its quietude save the mere distant echoes of the stirring public events of the day. The existence, however, in an island on Lochleven for so many centuries, of an ecclesiastical institution of so much importance and prominence, must necessarily have exercised a beneficial influence over the whole of the surrounding district; and to it is no doubt due the early erection of the three Churches which, from the dawn of Christianity in the eastern districts of Scotland, existed at Kinross, Orwell, and Portmoak. Situated as these churches were, on the very margin of Lochleven, they probably originated as mere primitive places of worship, where the monks of St Serf's could minister periodically to the spiritual wants of the people of the district. Viewed in this light, and regarded as the centre from which there first emanated and spread over the eastern and central counties of Scotland that doctrine which has done so much to purify and elevate humanity, the ruined and lonely Priory of St Serf's becomes an object of deep and very special national interest.

The protection of Lochleven Castle, if it did not lead to the original settlement of the Culdees on the adjacent Island of St Serf's, must certainly, by the fostering security it afforded, have tended to render the Priory there more permanent and prosperous; and probably to this cause may also be attributed the founding of the ancient Monastery said to have existed at Portmoak, and the Hospital at Scotlandwell, founded in 1238. In a similar manner the existence of "*the* Castle" seems to have led to the erection—within a four mile radius—of several interesting minor baronial residences, the ruins of which still adorn the district, and impart to it a romantic and old world interest, which, but for them, it would not have possessed. The principal of these interesting relics of days long gone by is Burleigh Castle, situated near to the north shore of Lochleven, which, for several generations formed the residence of the Barons of Burleigh, and the ruins of which now form, along with the ruins of Lochleven Castle, an interesting feature in the conjoined Baronies of Kinross and Burleigh, now vested in Sir Graham Graham Montgomery, Baronet, the present " Laird of Lochleven." To the east of Burleigh Castle there is still to be seen the ruined tower of Arnot, now belonging to Mr Bruce of Arnot, the lineal descendant of Sir William Bruce of Kinross, and which for many centuries belonged to the ancient family of " Arnots of that ilk ; " while to the west of Lochleven there are the picturesquely situated ruins of Dowhill Castle, the ancient seat of the Lindsays of Dowhill, a family which, in the reign of Queen Mary, occupied an important place in the county ;—Cleish Castle, once the residence of the Meldrums of Cleish and Barns, and afterwards of the Colvilles of Cleish, both of which families in their day bore no unimportant part in public affairs, and which now forms the residence of Mr Young of Cleish, the Convener of Kinross-shire ;—Aldie Castle, belonging to the Mercers of Aldie ;—and Tulliebole Castle, still forming the country seat of Lord Moncreiff, the present Lord Justice-Clerk, and representative of the old local family of Moncreiffs of Tulliebole. Studded as the county is with these interesting and picturesque old buildings, each nestling amid its appropriate clump of weird and gigantic trees, which for centuries has sheltered it from the wintry blast, it is difficult indeed to over-estimate the antiquarian and romantic interest they impart to the whole district. Each of these architectural relics of bygone days has its own peculiar associations, and its own special story, although these dwindle into vastly minor importance when compared with the historic associations circling around the venerable pile whose history forms the special subject of these pages.

CHAPTER II.

EARLY HISTORY OF THE CASTLE.

"O ! now doth death line his dead chaps with steel,
   The swords of soldiers are his teeth, his fangs ;
   And now he feasts, mousing the flesh of men,
   In undetermin'd differences of Kings."
                                        SHAKSPERE.

THE origin of Lochleven Castle is, on account of its extreme remoteness, involved in impenetrable obscurity. It is said to have been built during the Pictish period by Congal, King of the Picts, whose reign extended from 511 to 535 ; but if so, the original building must have been removed and replaced by one of much more modern construction. The keep or square tower as at present existing partakes of the Norman character, and was most probably erected during the eleventh or twelfth centuries. Originally this tower formed in all likelihood the only building on the Island ; and, with its encircling waters, its great massive walls, and having its only possible access perched some 25 feet above the ground level, it must have proved, against the then known modes of attack, an almost impregnable stronghold. No doubt, as time advanced, and as the necesssity for further accommodation led to the erection of buildings adjacent to and under the immediate protection of the keep, the necessity also arose for a surrounding rampart, enclosing and protecting the whole buildings. The ramparts are clearly of a more modern date than the "keep," and, from a very superficial examination of these, it is evident that various changes have from time to time been made on them in order to enlarge the enclosed space. These alterations have been made in a rough and ready way, which has rendered the walls somewhat rude and irregular, although they are certainly strong enough in structure.

The round tower in the south-east corner of the courtyard, and which now forms part of the ramparts, is clearly more modern than the ramparts themselves. It, as well as several of the more subordinate buildings in the courtyard, were probably erected in the early years of the sixteenth century, when considerable structural additions were made by Sir Robert Douglas, the then Laird of Lochleven, who was killed at the Battle of Pinkie in 1547. These alterations appear to have been made by Sir Robert immediately after his marriage—in or about the year 1533 — to Lady Margaret Erskine, daughter of John Lord Erskine ; for, among the debris, which, until within the last few years lay piled up in the courtyard, there was found a stone bearing the initials of " R · D · M · E."

The early historic references to "the Castle" are of a very meagre and incidental character, but, meagre and incidental as these are, they are sufficient to show that from a very early period it was dignified as one of the royal residences and national strongholds of Scotland ; and, from 1124 downwards, we find that it formed the occasional residence of the successive occupants of the Scottish throne. During the reign of David I., in a Parliament held in Scone, in the summer of 1368, a special inspection was ordered of the strongholds and means of defence throughout the country ; and in particular the Commissioners were directed to visit in the first instance, the four royal castles

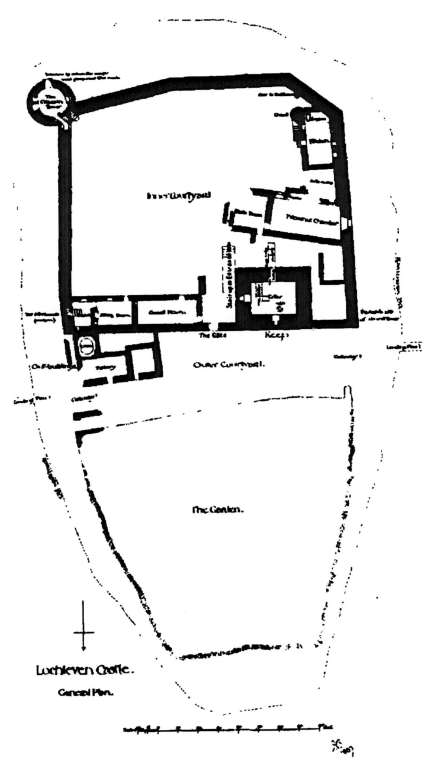

Inner Courtyard

Pleasance Chamber

Great Room

Keep

The Gate

Outer Courtyard

Out-buildings

The Garden

Lochleven Castle.

General Plan.

GROUND PLAN OF CASTLE ISLAND

of Lochleven, Edinburgh, Stirling, and Dumbarton (*"quatuor castra regia videlicet Lacus de Leuyn, Edynburgh, Strivelyn, et Dumbarton"*), and to give orders for their being at once repaired, garrisoned, and provided with victuals, warlike engines, and all other means necessary for resisting attack. This Parliamentary Commission was issued after the persistent attempts of Edward III. to subjugate Scotland ; and the fact that Lochleven occupies so prominent a place in the special instructions to the Commissioners, indicates in the most unmistakable manner the importance which was then attached to it. Probably the erection of the surrounding ramparts, and several of the subordinate buildings within the courtyard, formed the practical result of this tour of inspection, and the castle may then have assumed a form somewhat approaching that indicated by the existing ruins. These—as shown on the ground plan (Pl. II.) and other sketches illustrating these observations—consist of the well-known and familiar square massive keep occupying the north-east corner of the courtyard—a long range of buildings of substantial and, for the times, apparently comfortable construction extending from the entrance gateway all along the inside of the north rampart—the interesting round tower in the south-east corner of the courtyard, and a range of buildings, of which the character is unknown, extending along nearly the whole of the west rampart. Outside the courtyard there are the bakery and other inferior offices ; and these, and the enclosed garden, with the approaches to the entrance gate from the eastern and western shores, occupied the whole of the rest of the Island. Before the level of Lochleven was lowered by the extensive drainage operations of sixty years ago, by which the depth of the lake was reduced fully four and a half feet, the Castle Island, which is now five acres in extent, contained little more than two acres ; and, in considering many of the details introduced into these pages, it will be necessary to bear in view that at the time here treated of, the shore lay close to the base of the ramparts on the southern half of the island, and to the base of the low wall or terrace enclosing the garden on the northern half.

That the Castle was not infrequently used as a royal residence is proved by the fact that in the year 1256 Alexander III., then only sixteen years of age, and his still more juvenile Queen (daughter of the then King of England, Henry III.), while resident within its walls were seized by the Comyns, and carried by them prisoners to Stirling. This seizure was made under cover of night, and, from the manner in which it is referred to in history, it does not appear to have been attended with violence or bloodshed. Indeed, from the then state of public feeling and general dislike to the English influence which was exercised over the youthful King, it is more than probable that the object of the expedition was attained less by actual force than by moral suasion, and that Alexander himself was not an altogether unwilling captive in the hands of his subjects. Be that as it may, the Comyns, by their bold and masterly move, paralysed the efforts of the English king, and unintentionally paved the way to that period of national independence and of comparative peace and security, which only terminated when the unfortunate Scottish monarch lost his life thirty years afterwards, by the stumbling of his horse in the dark over a rock into the sea at Kinghorn. With the death of Alexander, and the succession of his infant granddaughter, the Maid of Norway, arose those troublous times, so quaintly depicted in the "Cantus" with which Wyntoun pathetically closes the 7th Book of his Cronykil :—

"Quhen Alyxander oure King was dede
That Scotland led in luve and le'
Away was sons off ale and brede
Off wyne and wax, off gamin and gle';

Oure gold was changyd into lede,
Cryst borne in to Vyrgynyte,
Succoure Scotland and remede
That state in its perplexyte."

In the struggles of the period extending from the death of Alexander to the defeat of the English at Bannockburn in 1314, the inhabitants of Kinross-shire bore their share, and the discordant notes of war and strife were not unheard amid the quiet solitudes of Lochleven. According to Balfour's "Annals," the Castle was besieged by the English in 1301, but the siege was immediately raised by Sir John Comyn, and in October 1303 the English King, Edward I., at the head of his victorious army, passed through Kinross on his way to Dunfermline, where he took up his winter quarters, after a successful raid in the more northern counties of Scotland. Nay, if "Blind Harry" is to be believed, the Castle during the same period formed the scene of one of the many brilliant exploits of our great national hero, Sir William Wallace. The following is a modernised paraphrase of the Lay in which the "Blind Minstrel" recounts the exploit :

"The Scots at large over-ran all Fife, and of Englishmen none were left in that country, but in Lochleven there lay a company upon that Inch in a small house they had prepared—Castle was none, but surrounded with water 'wicht.' Beside Crail Wallace assembled his men, his purpose being to essay Kinghorn, then held under the captaincy of a knight called Grey. By short notice Wallace resolved to carry out his purpose, ere Grey, by tidings from his King, could be led to reckon for such a pro-

ceeding on Wallace's part. Having taken that house, Wallace
little tarry made, and on the morning after, without more delay,
he crossed the moor to a tryst they had set, near Scotland Well,
where they their lodging took without hindrance. After supper
Wallace bade them go rest. 'Myself,' he said, 'will walk, I
think it may be best.' As he commanded they unwillingly
obeyed ; and while they slept, Wallace quickly armed himself
and passed to Lochleven near midnight, with eighteen men with
him whom he had warned carefully. These men knew well he
came to inspect the place. 'Fellows,' he said,' I wish to caution you.
Consider well this place and understand that it might do great
scaith to Scotland. If succour comes to them out of the south
they may take it in, and keep the place at their own will. Upon
yon Inch richt mony men may be ready to issue out whenever
they see a suitable time. We cannot risk to bide long here.
Yon folk have food, you may well trust, in abundance. Water
we cannot keep from them, and it therefore behoves us to adopt
some other wile. Ye shall remain here in silence at this port,
and I myself will bring the boat to you.' Therewith he in haste
cast off his clothes, saying, 'No watchman can I see on yon side.'
Holding on his sark, and having his good sword bound on his
neck, he then leaped into the flood, and over he swam, for hindrance
he found none. The boat he took and brought it to his men,
and having arrayed himself well, he would tarry no longer, but
embarking, he and his men rowed to the other side. The island
they took, drawn sword in hand, and spared none that they found
before them ; struck doors up, and stabbed men where they lay.
Upon the Southerns thus sadly they rushed. Thirty they slew
that were in the same place. To make defence the Englishmen
had no space. Their five women Wallace sent off that 'sted,'
woman nor bairn he never caused put to death, and the good they

took as it had been their own. Then Wallace said, ' Fellows I make you aware the provision that is within this store we will not lose—cause all to assemble at once. Cause warn Ramsay and our good men, every one, I will remain while this *"warnstor"* be gane. (Then) they sent forth a man, their horses put to keep drew up the boat, then took to their beds to sleep. Wallace's power, which lay near Scotlandwell, missed him away before the sun arose. Some made a moaning, and marvelled at the cause ; but Ramsay bade them cease and mourn nought for Wallace. ' It is for good that he is from us 'gone as ye shall see, trust well in truth. My head to pledge, Lochleven he passed to see, for, excepting those that are there, no Englishman know we in all this land betwixt these waters left. Tidings of him ye shall see soon hereafter.' As they among themselves talked in this wise, a message came and charged them to arise. ' My Lord,' said the messenger, ' to dinner has you called in to Lochleven, which is a Royal hold. Ye shall fare well, therefore put off all sorrow.' They armed themselves very early on the morrow, and thither past of Wallace to learn his will. Thus they assembled in a full blyth fellowship. They lodged there till eight days were ended. Of meat and drink they had enough and to spare. Brought out the gear the Southerns had brought there, caused the boat to be burnt, and then to St Johnston (Perth) they fared."

It may seem somewhat incongruous, in a narrative aspiring to be rigidly historical, to wander thus into the realms of poetic romance, still there is a fascination about the incident as narrated by the Blind Minstrel which renders impossible its exclusion. It is therefore given for what it is worth, and each must attach to it such credence as he thinks it deserves. There is certainly this to be said in its favour, that one can scarcely read the graphic and detailed account without feeling that it must have had some foundation in fact. Harry's Homeric effusion was not the mere offspring of his poetic fancy, but is in the main substantially in harmony with what is known of the prominent features of the career of the great Scottish Patriot and Champion. It is alleged, too, that he had for his guidance a record in writing, left by Wallace's secretary; and at all events, it is known that he amplified the narrative of his hero's exploits from local tradition picked up by him in his wanderings through the country little more than a century after Wallace's death. If at that time a tradition at all approaching in similarity to the incident as above narrated was current in the locality, we may credit it, at all events, to the extent of believing that the shores of Lochleven were actually trodden by the foot of the illustrious Scottish hero. It must be admitted, however, that the exploit is not alluded to in the historical records of the period; but in times so troublous and stirring, when the taking of a castle was an almost daily event, it is not to be wondered at if, amid more important occurrences of the same kind, the retaking of Lochleven Castle should have excited a mere temporary and local interest. We certainly find from authentic history that Wallace at the time referred to had returned from France, and that he was actively engaged in harassing the English invader in his attempt to retain his hold on Fifeshire, and the other districts he had conquered. In regard to the construction of Blind Harry's narrative, it will be noticed that there is some confusion between the two "inches" or "islands"—the Castle Island and St Serf's Island. The "Inch" from which Wallace brought the boat must be St Serf's, scarcely a mile distant from the shore at Scotlandwell, while the "Inch" to which he rowed his men must have been the Castle Island, as Wallace himself calls it a "Royal Hold" when he summons his men to join him. These errors and inconsistencies are common throughout the Minstrel's poem, and arise probably from his inability, owing to his blindness, to realise accurately the scene of the incidents he so graphically describes.

Quarter of a century after Wallace's death, Edward Baliol, on the succession of David I., the son of Robert the Bruce, attempted to usurp the throne of Scotland, and during the brief but sanguinary struggle—in which Baliol was powerfully aided by the English King, Edward III.—Lochleven Castle was stubbornly held in the interest of the Scottish King. It formed one of the only four castles which were retained by the supporters of King David, viz.:—Dumbarton, Lochleven, Kildrummie, and Urquhart, with the addition of the tower of Lochdowne. At that period Fife and Kinross and the southern portion of Perthshire formed the theatre of war, and Lochleven Castle appears to have been regarded by Baliol as far too important a stronghold to be allowed to remain in the hands of the Scottish patriotic faction. It was then under the governorship of Sir Allan Vipon, with whom was associated James Lamby, a citizen of St Andrews, and the task of besieging it was committed to Sir John Stryvelyne, a renegade Scotchman. The attacking force was chiefly English, but it seems to have included several prominent Scotchmen, who, like Stryvelyne, had followed Baliol's example, and sworn fealty to the English King; and among these are especially mentioned Michael of Arnot, Michael and David of Wemyss, and Richard the Melville. The siege seems to have been a protracted and serious one, commencing at "Myde-lentryn" (20th February 1335), and continuing till sometime after " Saynt Margret the Queny's day," (16th November), and during its course supports had to be frequently drafted from Perth, where a detachment of the English army was then stationed. Stryvelyne erected a fort of sods and earth in the Old Churchyard of Kinross, which, from its slightly elevated position, as well as from its immediate proximity to the loch, formed the most suitable place from which attempts could be made to harass and annoy the sturdy defenders of the Castle. Every effort was tried, by means of persistent attacks by boats, to surprise the garrison and storm the Castle; but after being repeatedly repulsed with great loss, the besiegers were compelled to adopt the more tedious process of reducing it by means of a strict blockade. Even this proved equally abortive, for the brave garrison, taking advantage of Stryvelyne's absence at Dunfermline with "all the gentlys that with him were," attending a religious festival on Saint Margaret's day, made a secret and well-planned sortie; and having attacked their besiegers, captured the fort which they had erected, drove them with great slaughter from their position, and carried off their whole stores and everything else that their boats could carry to the Castle, including—

> ".   .   .   All ryches
> That to their lykyn pleasand wes
> Alblastrys (*crossbows*) and bowys off vyse
> And all thing that mycht mak serwyse
> Or helpe thame into pres of were."

The news of the capture of his fort was no doubt sad intelligence for Sir John Stryvelyne, when it was conveyed to him at Dunfermline; and we are not surprised when we are told that he was "*nerrare wade than wrathe, and swore mony ane awfull athe,*" and resumed the siege with a firm resolve not to desist until he had won the Castle and put the whole of its garrison to the sword. The continued siege, however, was attended with no better success; for after some time, during which the besiegers were exposed to great peril, owing to incessant attacks from the garrison, Stryvelyne was at length forced to abandon his attempt, and the worthy Wyntoun indulges in an almost audible literary chuckle as he leads him discomfited off the stage—

> " Swa sune owt off the land gat he
> Wyth a fere grettare schame
> Then he browcht wyth hym fra hame."

This reverse, coupled with the troubles and annoyances which the English were simultaneously encountering in other parts of Scotland, seems to have led to a concentration of the English forces, and the Castle was allowed to remain in the hands of the supporters of its rightful owner, the Scottish king. It is noted in relation to this siege that it forms the first occasion in which the name of "Douglas"—which afterwards, for many generations, formed the family name of the "Lairds of Lochleven"—became connected in history with the Castle, one of its prominent defenders during the siege being Sir John Douglas of Dalkeith, believed to be a younger brother of the famous "Knight of Liddesdale." Apparent relics of this siege are still to be seen at Kinross House, in the shape of large roughly formed bullets of stone, fully nine inches in diameter, of which several were found half a century ago in close proximity to the Castle and to the site of the fort on the Kinross shore, after the loch was lowered by the drainage operations already referred to. These bullets were presumably projected from culverins, which had only recently come into use in England, and which were no doubt used by Edward in his military operations in Scotland at this time.

For nearly half a century after the siege the Castle was entrusted to the care of various successive Castellans; and it seems to have been kept mainly for State purposes, and was not infrequently utilised as a place of imprisonment for important

political offenders.   Thus, in 1368, it became for a considerable
period the place of captivity of the Steward of Scotland—who
afterwards became King Robert II.—and of his son, the notorious
" Wolf of Badenoch."   Robert was nephew to the then reigning
king—David II. ; and the rigorous measures which the king
adopted against his nephew and grand-nephew appear to have
been instigated by David's plebeian (second) wife, Margaret
Logie, to whom the Steward and his son had rendered themselves obnoxious.   The exact length of their detention in the
Castle cannot be ascertained, but apparently it began early in
1368, and only terminated on the divorce of the queen at Lent
in the following year, when the offenders were restored to the
royal favour.   By the death of David, in 1370, Robert, the
ci-devant captive, succeeded to the throne ; and apparently his
former experiences within the walls of Lochleven Castle had not
been so unpleasant as to prevent him from regarding and treat-
ing it somewhat in the light of a " pet possession."   At all
events, in 1372, we find him bestowing it as a mark of affection
on " Eufamie Ross," his second wife, and David, Earl of Strath-
earn, their eldest son, under the description, "*Castri nostri lacus
de Levyn cum pertinen ;*" and eighteen years later, on the occasion
of the marriage of his niece, King Robert again conveys it by
charter dated 1390 to his niece's husband, Sir Henry Douglas,
second son of the Sir John Douglas of Dalkeith who had distinguished himself at the defence of the Castle in 1335.   From
this date Lochleven formed, for three centuries and a half, the
patrimonial estate of Sir Henry and his descendants, who
adopted the territorial title of " Douglas of Lochleven."   Apparently the office of Castellan formed a hereditary office attached
as a pertinent to the estate ; for even after the proprietorship of
the lands became vested in the Douglases, the Crown continued

to hold, and occasionally to exercise, a right to use the Castle for State purposes. Thus, in 1478, it was assigned as the prison of the "unfortunate and virtuous" Patrick Graham, first Archbishop of St Andrews, who died within its walls that year. He was an eminent dignitary of the Scottish Church, who, on account of some undefined ecclesiastical offence, was sent to a cell in St Columba, in the Isle of Iona, and shortly afterwards was removed to the Monastery of Dunfermline; but as he was found "to aim again at the world," his persecutors "shutts him up close in the Castle of Lochleven, where he died, and was interred in St Servanus' Isle there." Until within the last few years considerable doubt existed as to the site of Archbishop Graham's grave; but in course of an exploration made by the Society of Antiquaries, within the ruined chapel on St Serf's, he was found interred near to the supposed site of the altar. The bones were in a good state of preservation, and indicated a man of about five feet ten inches in height. At the same time, and immediately beneath the Archbishop's remains, there were found the remains of St Ronan, "a man of admirable sanctity," who, in 930, was appointed Abbot of St Serf's, and lived and died there in a full age. These two bodies formed the only interments within the chapel, the ordinary burying-ground being outside the chapel walls; and it was reasonably conjectured that they must be the remains of the only two men of marked distinction who are recorded to have been interred on St Serf's. The appearance, too, of the remains corresponded generally with the periods at which the deaths respectively occurred.

The last captive of historic note who was consigned to the Castle was Thomas Percy, Earl of Northumberland, when he fled from England to escape the vengeance of Queen Elizabeth, vainly hoping to find refuge and protection in Scotland. Falling into the hands of the Regent Moray, in 1569, the distinguished refugee was subjected to rigorous imprisonment in Lochleven Castle for upwards of three years, when he was basely surrendered to the implacable English Queen by Moray's successor in the regency, Morton. The earl was taken direct from the Castle to York, where, a few days afterwards, he was executed, without even the form of trial. His treacherous betrayal and sad fate form the subject of one of the most interesting and touching of the Border Ballads, although the characters and local incidents introduced are more or less imaginary.

The impression that the Castle, while in the hands of the Douglas family, was to some extent regarded rather as State than as private property, is strengthened by the fact that there existed at and prior to the sixteenth century, a separate family residence, close to the western shore of Lochleven, and in nearest possible proximity to the Castle. This building, which is described by Sir Robert Sibbald, in his "History of Fife and Kinross," as "a neat manour," bore the name of "New House of Lochleven," and it was only demolished in the early portion of last century. From an exploration made a few months ago, it was found to have been situated to the north of the north-east corner of the present garden at the back of Kinross House; indeed, part of the wall of that garden seems to have been the original enclosing wall of the lawn or garden in front of "the manour." Like the present house, "the manour" appears to have stood with its back towards the Loch; and all along the back of the building there has evidently been a range of offices facing the Loch, which, judging from the pavement still existing, had been used as stables in connection with the house.

CHAPTER III.

QUEEN MARY AT LOCHLEVEN.

"Stern Ruin's ploughshare drives elate
Full on thy bloom."

BURNS.

THE early historic incidents already narrated, although of undoubted importance, lose much of their interest when contrasted
with the occurrences within and around the walls of Lochleven
Castle during the reign of the lovely but unfortunate Mary
Stuart, Queen of Scotland. It is on this brief but stirring
epoch that the student of Scottish history invariably finds his
attention chiefly rivetted, and it is to the associations of this
period that Lochleven Castle is indebted for that deep historic interest which encircles its ruins. The hapless Queen's
association with the Castle was not, as we are apt to suppose,
limited merely to the term of her long imprisonment there, but
extends over the greater part of the brief but eventful seven
years which constituted the whole duration of her career as
Queen of Scotland. Seven years does not form a very
lengthened period in an average life, and even of her short life
it did not constitute a large proportion, and yet, brief as it is,
one feels bewildered in recalling the many important and tragic
events which occurred within its limits.

On the 15th day of August 1561, she—a widowed Queen

at the early age of eighteen years—bade adieu for ever to France, where her earlier years had been spent amidst luxuries, pleasures, and refinements well calculated to make her life there, as it really appears to have been, a bright and happy one. Within five days she landed, in a cold and chilling Scotch mist, on the bare and rugged shores of her native country, and, amid great public rejoicings assumed her powers and duties and responsibilities as Queen of Scotland, surrounded by as motley a crowd of courtiers and advisers as ever yet encircled a throne—courtiers and advisers who, with but few exceptions, had one feeling, and one feeling only, in common, a rapacious and unscrupulous desire for their own personal aggrandisement. Periodical excursions through the outlying counties of Scotland, varied by residences of longer or shorter duration in Edinburgh, where she was engrossed either in adjusting the dissensions which were perpetually arising among her turbulent courtiers—in conducting long religious controversies with the inflexible reformer, John Knox—in finessing with her powerful and jealous kinswoman, Queen Elizabeth, or in receiving and disposing of the numerous and brilliant offers of marriage which literally flowed in upon her, sufficiently occupied the first three years of her residence in Scotland. Then transpired her fatal marriage with the weak, vain, and unprincipled Darnley, followed almost immediately by jealousy, distrust, and ultimate estrangement between them—the revolt of her disaffected nobles promptly subdued by the Queen taking the field in person at the head of her army—the assassination of her confidential secretary, Rizzio, at Darnley's instigation in March 1566, culminating in the barbarous murder of Darnley himself in February 1567, or little more than eighteen months after he had become the Queen's husband—her brief widowhood of three months terminating in her marriage with Bothwell—the very man who, as she had only too good reason to know, had been the prime mover in the assassination of her unworthy husband—the immediate revolt once more of the principal nobility—the marshalling of the opposing forces at Carberry Hill, and the avoidance of a hostile collision at the last moment by the flight of Bothwell, and the surrender of the Queen to the confederate Lords—her return to Edinburgh not as a sovereign, but as a prisoner in the hands of her turbulent subjects—her secret and hasty removal to Lochleven Castle—her year of rigorous imprisonment there—her romantic escape and last rallying effort on the disastrous field of Langside, and—closing event of all— her marvellous flight across the border, only to receive at the hands of the remorseless Queen of England, harsher and yet more cruel treatment than she would have met with at the hands of the rudest and most unscrupulous of her own subjects.

In glancing thus briefly over the more prominent events of Queen Mary's short but stirring public life, it is well that it does not fall within the scope of these observations to enter upon the much debated question of her guilt or innocence of the revolting crimes which have been charged against her. That question has engaged the attention of men of various nationalities during the past three centuries, and countless volumes in many different languages have been devoted to its discussion, and still no really convincing solution on either side has been attained, for the obvious reason, that there is an undoubted element of truth on both sides. On the one hand her warmest defender must allow that there was a reckless and headstrong, if not criminal blindness in the fatal manner in which she, in the midst of her personal trials and perplexities surrendered herself to the dictates of her impulsive passionate nature; and on the other hand her bitterest detractor must admit that her character was subjected to the basest and most systematic vilification by her enemies, and that in order to preclude her from ever regaining her regal power, they did not scruple by forgery and otherwise, to try to convert what was at the best only reasonable and natural suspicion into absolute and incontrovertible proof.

Whether she is regarded as guilty or innocent it must be conceded that the unfortunate circumstances under which she made her public advent in this country were of a character as overwhelming as they were varied and complex. She was unfortunate in her French extraction and early education and training, as it placed her out of direct sympathy with the tastes and feelings and habits of the people over whom she was called upon to rule, and she was doubly unfortunate in her devotion to Roman Catholicism, considering the peculiar religious crisis during which she assumed the reins of government, but she was most unfortunate of all in her entire dependence for counsel and guidance upon nobles whose scheming and unscrupulous character constitutes a dark and indelible blot on the fair annals of Scotland. When, in her youth and inexperience, she embarked on her public career in this country, she was thrown into a state of society for which she was in every way unsuited—or rather which was utterly unsuited for her—and the distinguished graces of mind and person with which she was so strikingly gifted, coupled with her impulsiveness of disposition and gaiety of character and manner, only added to the many complications and difficulties which so quickly gathered around her. Whatever may have been her sins and errors she amply suffered for them by her long cheerless imprisonment, and by her deeply tragic death, and those have long since become obscured in the halo of romantic interest with which time has encircled her. In no history, sacred or profane, ancient or modern, is there to be found any human character so thoroughly calculated to stir our warmest sympathies, or to engross our deepest interest, and age after age as it passes, only seems to make her, and the tragic events of her career, a more and more fascinating and prominent historical feature. How strikingly does her memory contrast in these days with the memory of her immaculate and powerful kinswoman and enemy, Queen Elizabeth. Time seldom fails to work out its own revenge, and, when it does work it out, it certainly makes it, as in this instance, a complete and an overwhelming one.

It is evident that, from the time of Queen Mary's arrival in Scotland, Lochleven formed one of her favourite places of resort. Within a month of her landing on the Scottish shores, we find her making a seventeen days' tour through the central counties, remaining for a night and sometimes longer at the principal places in her route. On the 11th of September she and her retinue, consisting of fifteen of the ladies of her household, six of the members of her Council, her uncle the Marquis d'Elbœuf, and her illegitimate brother, James Stuart, afterwards Earl of Moray, left Edinburgh for Linlithgow, and the day after proceeded to Stirling. On the 15th the gay and brilliant cavalcade left Stirling and rode by Alloa, Culross, and Inverkeithing to Leslie Castle, the seat of the Earl of Rothes, where she passed the night. On this occasion part of her route lay along the shores of Lochleven, and she must then, for the first time have seen, if she did not actually visit, Lochleven Castle. Exactly a fortnight afterwards we find her and her retinue again passing along the margin of the Loch on their return from Falkland to Edinburgh. On this occasion (29th September) it is more than probable that she broke her journey at the Castle in passing. Situated nearly midway between Falkland and Queensferry it was undoubtedly the most convenient spot to select as a temporary halting place, and no doubt the inhabitants of the county of Kinross were then afforded, for the first time, an opportunity of gazing upon their youthful and fascinating Queen, and of contributing towards those hearty demonstrations of loyalty which everywhere were showered upon her, and which gratified her so much in this, her first visit to the rural districts of her realm.

At this period the Castle, although "a part and pertinent" of the Estate of Lochleven, was apparently still regarded to some extent as Crown property; it was committed to the care of Lady Margaret Douglas of Lochleven, the widow of Sir Robert Douglas, who, fourteen years previously, had fallen at the Battle of Pinkie. Lady Margaret, as already mentioned, was a daughter of John Lord Erskine, and sister of the then Earl of Mar. At the time of her marriage to Sir Robert Douglas, she had stooped to the dishonour of becoming one of the rather numerous mistresses of Queen Mary's father, James V., and had born to him a son—James Stuart, who, as Earl of Moray, was fated to exercise a powerful influence not only on the future of his country, but also on the ultimate destiny of his royal but unfortunate sister. The exact date of Moray's birth history leaves open to doubt, but it is generally believed to have occurred in or near 1533, and, at the date when his sister took possession of the throne of her fathers, he must therefore have been about twenty-eight years of age. The exact date of his mother's marriage to Sir Robert Douglas is also a point which history fails to fix, some historians actually alleging that it took place previous to Moray's birth. It is certainly clear that, at the utmost, Moray, at the date of his mother's marriage, must have been a mere infant, for at the time of Queen Mary's first visit to Lochleven, Lady Margaret Douglas had resident in her household there not fewer than ten children, the youngest of whom must at least have been fully fourteen years of age, and her eldest son, Sir William Douglas, could not, therefore, have been more than a year or two younger than his illegitimate brother, Moray. Clearly no lengthened period could have elapsed between the birth of Moray, and the marriage of his mother to Sir Robert Douglas, and it is quite possible that the marriage may have actually occurred previous to his birth. The subject is anything but a pleasing one to contemplate, and, although considerable allowance falls to be made for the corrupt and licentious character of the times, yet the light in which it presents Lady Margaret is certainly not calculated to prepossess historians in her favour—indeed, it has naturally had a powerful effect in the opposite direction, and for her may not unreasonably be claimed the distinction of being the " best abused " woman in Scottish history. Historians—especially those favourable to Queen Mary—seem to vie with each other in depicting Lady Margaret's character and disposition in the darkest possible shades, and yet, if the real truth were known, it would probably be found that, in the midst of all her frailty she still retained much of womanly tenderness and feeling, as well as of patrician dignity and honour. The following touching extract from a letter written by her to the Countess of Moray, her daughter-in-law, on the occasion of the death of her little grandchild, sufficiently shows that whatever her past life may have been, she was anything but an unloving or unsympathetic woman.

" Efter maist hartlie commendatioun, this is to advertis your Ladyschip that it has pleasit God to tak your doichtor, my bairne, to Himself, quhilk is the graetest greif that ever came to my hertt for ony of hir yiers outher of my awin beiring or of any utheris.   Nocht the less I man gif thankis to God as I have done in greittar matters . . . I pray your Ladyschip to be of good comfort and treitt yourself weill that ye may live to bring up the lief to be honest folkis, for naebody has gotten the greittest loss bot I.   I dout nocht but God sall send your Ladyschip bairnis after this, to do you plessour, for ye are young eneuch, but thair is nayn abill to do me sic plessour as sche did, but I commit all things to the plessour of God quha conserve you eternalie."

Even in her treatment of Queen Mary, Lady Douglas seems, notwithstanding all that has been written to the contrary, to have shown a singular freedom from harshness or injustice, if we consider the crucial circumstances under which they were latterly thrown together, and more especially the very peculiar relationship (?) which existed between them.   The alleged cruelty of Lady Douglas towards her unfortunate Sovereign seems to owe its origin more to literary imagination than to literal fact, and in Queen Mary's correspondence, as well as in other contemporary writings, there is not only no imputation tending to support the accusation, but, on the contrary, much that tends to prove that Lady Douglas's feelings towards her unhappy captive were far from being altogether devoid either of sympathy, or of womanly pity.   Indeed, it rather appears that Sir Walter Scott, with that intuitive perception which always distinguishes the genuine artist, has in "The Abbot" depicted Lady Margaret Douglas in her true colours—as a lady of recognised ability and great force of character, clinging in the most trying circumstances and in spite of her own unworthy antecedents, to that *noblesse oblige*, which, as a general rule, is the natural accompaniment of patrician birth.

Whether or not Lochleven Castle was visited on the occasion of the Queen's first tour through the central provinces of her kingdom, it is clear that shortly after her return to Scotland, she, in the course of her long and frequent excursions to Fife and Kinross, repeatedly took up her abode within its walls for the purpose of enjoying her favourite sport of hawking, and that she even fitted up a presence chamber there, and provided other apartments, for the purpose of adapting it, as far as possible, not merely for her own temporary occupation, but actually for State receptions. These apartments, according to the State records of the period, appear to have been fitted up in something like regal magnificence and comfort. The walls of her presence chamber and bedroom were decorated with ten pieces of tapestry illustrative of hunting and hawking—her bed was of green velvet fringed with silk, and made in the form of a chapel, the counterpane being of green taffeta—and her board cloth was green velvet lined with green taffeta. The canopy of the throne in her presence chamber was covered with crimson satin figured with gold, with its draperies fringed with gold and silver silk. Part of the furnishings of her chamber, consisting of a small sofa of ebony, and several chairs, are still to be seen at Dalmahoy, in the possession of the Earl of Morton, the lineal descendant of " Douglas of Lochleven." That these early royal residences within the Castle were more than mere short and passing visits, is further evidenced by the state preparations which were made for her reception, and by the following entries in the Inventory of movables of the Earl of Moray occurring under date 1561 (the year of her return from France):—
" four dossin of pewtar plaittis dalivarit to George Hog, to take to Loich Levyn at the Queenes coming there," and also " four dossin quhyt irne plaittis, and four courtings of yellow

C

tafiteis with ane frontell of the samyn." It is also stated that
there was found in the land reclaimed from the Loch, a small
sceptre with a carved stem hilted with ivory and mounted with
silver, which is supposed to have formed part of her travelling
regalia. To this period too may probably be assigned some of
the more modern buildings in the courtyard of the Castle, for it
is not unreasonable to suppose that the provision made by the
Queen for her own comfort and accommodation would not be
limited to the mere internal furnishing, but would also include
structural alterations of a more or less extensive character. In
particular, it may be regarded as a plausible conjecture that the
building within the courtyard, lying on the south side of the
square tower, may have been erected at this time for the special
purpose of being used as her presence chamber. The ruins of
this building have always formed an interesting archæological
puzzle, for they clearly indicate a room intended for public,
rather than for domestic use, and many visitors persist in
regarding it as the ruins of the chapel attached to the Castle.
For this belief there appear to be no grounds whatever, and it
is refuted by the fact that it has not, as it certainly would have
had, a window looking to the east, and that it has, as it is most
unlikely it would have had, a hearth and fire-place in its south
wall. This building, whatever its purpose, consisted of only one
spacious apartment, thirty-three feet in length and about eighteen
feet in breadth. It is only one storey in height, and the ceiling
must have been fully fourteen feet from the floor, while the
recesses for the windows and fire-place have plain but boldly
cut mouldings run round them, indicating a design to give something like imposing effect to the internal aspect of the room.
It has, too, a large window in its west gable wall, incorporated
in the western rampart, and thus afforded an extensive view

Plate III

BIRDS-EYE VIEW OF LOCHLEVEN CASTLE.

(restored)

Page 36.

across the loch towards Kinross and onwards over the long level strath to the Ochils near Stirling. It is not improbable, too, that the interesting round tower in the south-east corner of the courtyard, if not forming part of Sir Robert Douglas's alterations five-and-twenty years previously, may have been erected at this time. For some reason, never satisfactorily explained, this tower has always been locally known as "the Glassin Tower," and sometimes "the Glass Tower," and alike in its character and construction it is as peculiar as it is interesting. It contains only two apartments, exclusive of one in the roof, to which access could only be had from the ramparts. The apartment on the ground floor is a public room of small dimensions but of a superior and slightly ornate character, as it possesses a large cheerful window facing the south, projecting out from the wall and opening from the ceiling down to the very floor. The one above (which may have been sub-divided) is a bed-chamber, and has two shallow alcoves or recesses in the wall for bedsteads. The access to these two rooms is by a door-way leading direct from the courtyard into a small lobby, on one side of which there is a short flight of stone steps leading to the sleeping apartment above. If erected at the period suggested, this tower may have owed its origin simply to the Queen's desire to provide for herself, during her temporary residences within the Castle, suitable private apartments, without encroaching on the accommodation in the square tower required by Lady Douglas and her somewhat numerous house-hold.

The first of the royal visits of which there is any special historical record is in the spring of 1563, being about a year and a half after her arrival from France. On that occasion the Queen rode from Falkland to Lochleven on the 9th of April, and she remained until the 15th, when she rode back to Falkland, dining at Strathendry in passing. On the 13th April she is waited upon, while resident in the Castle, by the redoubtable Scotch Reformer, John Knox, who was deputed by the General Assembly to expostulate with her as to the laxity with which the recently enacted penal statutes were enforced against the Roman Catholics. Knox arrived at the Castle in the afternoon, and had a two hours' conference with the Queen before supper (seven o'clock). This was one of the many long and unprofitable discussions which she had with Knox on this constantly recurring ground of complaint, in the course of which she pleaded, but pleaded in vain, with the fearless and unyielding Reformer, that the same religious toleration should be extended to herself and her Roman Catholic subjects as she was herself prepared to extend to her Protestant subjects. The interview appears to have been conducted by the Queen with much spirit and ability, and at the same time with wonderful moderation and self-control, considering that Knox not only justified fearlessly his peremptory demands, but even indicated, in the sturdiest and plainest possible language, that the sword of State was entrusted to her by God to the end that justice might be done, and that if she failed to do her duty, others must do it for her. "Your subjects," he said, "crave from you protection and defence against evil-doers, but if you deny your duty unto them, do you expect to receive full confidence from them? I fear, madam, you shall not." The Queen, although naturally much irritated at Knox's sturdy and rigid definition of the scriptural duty of princes, does not appear to have retained any permanent feeling of resentment; for, before sunrise next morning, she sent Walter Melville and another messenger from Lochleven Castle to Kinross, where Knox was passing the night, summoning Knox to meet her again that day be-west the town of Kinross, where she was to be engaged hawking. This second interview with Knox, according to generally accepted local tradition, took place at Turfhills; and on this occasion the vexed subject of religious toleration does not appear to have been specially introduced. On the contrary, her chief object in wishing for a further interview with Knox seems to have been to enlist his aid in her efforts to allay some domestic differences between the Countess of Argyle and the Earl of Argyle, her husband. The Countess was an illegitimate sister of the Queen, and as she and her husband were Protestants and members of Knox's congregation, it was hoped that his influence might restore peace and harmony between the Earl and his wife. It is supposed that on this occasion the Queen graciously presented Knox with a small watch fitted in a crystal case of an oblong octagonal shape, as a mark of royal favour; and this watch, when M'Crie's "Life of Knox" was written, was still in the possession of a family in Aberdeenshire.

The next historical notice of Queen Mary's presence in Kinross-shire is of a much more dramatic and sensational character. The announcement of her matrimonial engagement with Darnley in July 1565 caused a considerable flutter of anger, jealousy, and excitement, both at the English Court and also among the Scottish nobles—Moray in particular being bitterly opposed to it, although he had originally favoured the alliance to the utmost of his power. Queen Elizabeth was then advocating, in her own peculiarly crooked and vacillating way, the pretensions of her own favourite courtier, Lord Robert Dudley, Earl of Leicester, as a suitor for Queen Mary's hand; and she was so enraged at the rumoured acceptance of Darnley, that she caused Lady Lennox (Darnley's mother) to be imprisoned in the Tower of London, and peremptorily recalled Darnley and his father, the

Earl of Lennox, to England. This summons Darnley and his father refused to obey; and Queen Elizabeth, with her usual propensity for scheming, entered into a plot with her ever ready and willing tool the Earl of Moray, along with other similarly disaffected Scotch Lords, to have Darnley and his father seized by force and transported to England. Into this scheme Moray, alike from his desire to gratify the English Queen, and from the strong personal dislike he now entertained towards Darnley, entered heartily; and, with the aid of his brother-in-law, the Earl of Argyle, the Earl of Rothes, and the Duke of Chatelherault, a plot was carefully devised for waylaying and seizing the Queen and Darnley, with the intention of conveying Darnley and his father to England, as required by Queen Elizabeth, and handing them over to her tender mercies; while the Queen herself was to be carried to Lochleven Castle and detained there under the care of Lady Douglas, Moray's mother, until at all events the conspirators had secured immunity from their daring act of violence and disloyalty.

The Queen and Darnley, as betrothed lovers, or rather as husband and wife, for a secret marriage had actually been solemnised between them in Rizzio's apartment in Stirling Castle in the second week of the previous April, were then making a gay and joyous tour through the central Scotch counties, accompanied by a brilliant retinue ; and the conspirators having ascertained that the Queen and her companion were to leave Perth on the morning of Sunday the 1st July 1565, at ten o'clock, and ride to Callender House by Queensferry, arranged that Rothes, with a band of followers, was to lie in wait for them at Parnwell, three miles to the south of Kinross, at a point where the then existing public thoroughfare, after skirting closely round the western base of Benarty, dips into a hollow near Blair-Adam.

The spot where this seizure was intended to be effected is still indicated by a Memorial Bridge spanning the old road from Queensferry to Perth, which was erected about seventy years ago by the Hon. William Adam of Blair-Adam, a proprietor in the immediate locality, and a most distinguished and enthusiastic antiquary. It was also arranged that Argyle was to come from Castle Campbell, at Dollar, with his followers to aid Rothes in his attempt to secure the person of the Queen, and thereafter to convey Darnley and Lennox to Castle Campbell, where they were to be detained till arrangements could be made for transporting them to England. Moray's part of the programme was simply to lie in wait within Lochleven Castle, and secure the safe detention of his royal sister there, and for this purpose he had made ample provision in the shape of an abundance of artillery and ammunition.

Never was act of treason more carefully planned, and no one who knows the locality can for a single moment doubt that it would (but for a most providential intervention) have proved entirely successful. The ordinary royal attendants were not very numerous, and even if they had resisted, which in the circumstances was more than doubtful, they would easily have been overpowered by the vastly superior force which Moray, Rothes, and Argyle had under their command. The risk, too, which the conspirators incurred in the enterprise was far more apparent than real. They had the power of Queen Elizabeth at their back, and with Darnley (Queen Mary's lover) and his father in Queen Elizabeth's hands, and Queen Mary herself safely immured in Lochleven Castle, their own safety was a mere matter of negotiation. They were besides in desperate straits, for they must have felt that in any event, and at the very worst, their position could not be more unfavourable as outlaws than it

was likely to become with Darnley as the husband and sole
adviser of their Sovereign.

As often happens in the most carefully devised schemes, a
totally unforeseen circumstance upset the whole plan at the
last moment, and it is alike interesting and gratifying to find
that the Queen owed her escape on this occasion to the loyalty
and devotion of a Kinross-shire Laird. Squire Lindsay of
Dowhill, whose residence, Dowhill Castle, is within a mile of
the spot where the seizure was proposed to be made, had by
some means discovered, late in the Saturday afternoon, the plot
that was being so carefully matured. Probably he or some of his
servants may have had their suspicions aroused by the premature
arrival of some of Rothes's adherents at the scene of the contemplated ambuscade. At all events he took horse late on Saturday
evening, and rode straight to Perth, a distance of fully twenty
miles, for the purpose of apprising the Queen of her danger.
By the time Lindsay reached the house in Perth in which she
was residing, she had retired for the night, but on his importun-
ate demand for an audience he was admitted to her chamber, and
disclosed to her the deeply laid scheme. With her usual prompti-
tude and energy, the Queen seized time by the forelock, and
raising her followers, she, accompanied by Darnley and his father,
left Perth at five o'clock on the Sunday morning, instead of ten,
as she had originally fixed for her departure, and she rode
through Kinross and past the appointed place of rendezvous
several hours before Rothes and Argyle were there to intercept
her, and long before Moray himself, from his mother's insular
stronghold, had begun his anxious watch for her appearance.
Argyle, we find, duly arrived at Kinross at the time appointed,
but it was only to learn that the royal cavalcade had passed two
hours before; and he coolly explained the cause of his journey by

saying that he came to pay his respects to his Sovereign, as he supposed she would remain at least to dine at Lochleven Castle.

The Queen's escort on this occasion was exceptionally strong, consisting not only of her own personal retinue and the followers of Lennox and Darnley, but also of 300 men hastily mustered in Perth by Lord Ruthven and others to act as a special bodyguard against the risk of attack by the way. One can imagine the stir which the progress of so large a mounted force would make as they, about seven o'clock in the still and peaceful Sabbath morning, rode rapidly along the "Old Back Causeway," which was then the thoroughfare through the town of Kinross ; and no doubt it formed the theme for much wonder, speculation, and remark, on the part of the villagers as they assembled that day for public worship in the quiet rural church on the shores of the placid lake. The town of Kinross at this time was little better than a village, containing a population of about 300, and consisting of not more than a hundred houses clustering close to the shore of the loch at and to the north-west of Sandport.

On the failure of their treasonable plot, Moray and Argyle retired into Lochleven Castle for a time ; but relying on Queen Elizabeth's promises, and the encouragement held out to them by her powerful minister Cecil, they, in a short time, rallied their forces and openly took up arms in the west. Queen Mary and Darnley, immediately after the public celebration of their marriage on the 29th July, adopted prompt and energetic measures against their rebel subjects ; and as the latter found themselves not only deluded by the English promises, but also unsupported by the general feeling of the country, the incipient rebellion was very speedily and easily crushed, and Moray and his companions were driven into exile, from which they were only recalled in the spring of the following year, when the assassination of Rizzio, and the base and cowardly treachery of Darnley caused the unhappy Queen in her bewilderment and perplexity to turn once more to her scheming and unscrupulous brother for counsel and guidance.

Two months after she had foiled Moray and his co-conspirators at Parnwell we find the Queen again at Lochleven Castle. On this occasion she and Darnley, at the head of an armed force, were making a triumphal progress through Fife, for the purpose of compelling all the known participators in the recent plot to give substantial and satisfactory security for their future loyalty. After securing possession of Castle Campbell, Lochleven Castle was the next place they turned their attention to, and on the 9th September its surrender was demanded at the hands of Lady Margaret Douglas, and of her eldest son Sir William Douglas, who had, about seventeen years previously, succeeded his father as "Laird of Lochleven." Sir William was by this time married to Lady Agnes Leslie, daughter of the Earl of Rothes, and he was thus, alike by relationship and marriage, closely connected with the prime movers in the recent plot. The royal demand for the surrender of the Castle does not seem to have been made in a very peremptory fashion ; for, on its being represented to the Queen that Sir William Douglas was suffering from illness, and that the Countess of Buchan, who was married to Sir William's younger brother Robert, had just been confined of her first child within the Castle, the Queen, with a leniency which was scarcely to be looked for in the circumstances, not only allowed Lady Margaret and her family to remain in undisturbed possession, but even condescended to dine at the Castle along with Darnley, before resuming their progress through Fifeshire.

After the public celebration of her marriage with Darnley in July 1565, we have, with the exception of the visit on 9th September of that year, to which reference has already been made, no record of the Queen's presence in Kinross-shire until she was brought to Lochleven Castle as a prisoner, in June 1567. No one can study the details of these sad and eventful two years, without feeling that she had, in her own harassing cares and trials, and in the plotting and counterplotting by which she was surrounded, more than sufficient to engross her every thought. In that period, brief as it was, there was condensed an amount of trial and bitter experience rarely found even in the longest and saddest life ; and yet, amid all her distracting anxieties, her quiet and pleasant retreat at Lochleven does not appear to have been altogether forgotten. We certainly find at all events that the district had, in the autumn of 1566, become so familiar and attractive to Darnley as to induce him to select it as his place of resort during one of those ever recurring fits of childish petulance and displeasure which so frequently led him to withdraw himself from Court and from his wife's society. The Queen at that time was lying seriously ill at Jedburgh, while Darnley was residing at Burleigh Castle, the Baronial residence of Lord Burleigh, situated close to the northern shore of Lochleven, and was apparently engrossed in his self-assumed duties as state gamekeeper within the county of Kinross. A letter written by Darnley at this period, dated from Burleigh Castle, and addressed to Sir William Douglas, affords an amusing glimpse of the imperious and inflated style in which the vain and infatuated youth assumed his newly acquired " regal " dignity and deportment :—

" LAIRD OF LOWGHE LEVYN—Whereas we have taken order through our realm for restraint of shooting with guns, you being Sheriff of those parts we will and command you hereby to apprehend all persons within your charge that so uses to shoot contrary to our order, and we having already understanding of one John Shawe, sun to Maister William Shawe, to be a common shooter, we also charge you hereby to take the said John and send him to us with his gun wherever we chance to be within three days after this present.   And further we being informed of divers fires used to be made upon the waters for fishing scareth the fowles, our pleasure is also that ye restrain all such fires being made till ye farther understand from us.   In all which doing these signed with our hands shall be your sufficient warrant against all persons.   Given at Burley this Wednesday, 11th of November.   Henry R."

"To our well-beloved the Laird of Lowghe Levyn."

CHAPTER IV.

QUEEN MARY'S IMPRISONMENT.

"   .   .   .   .   .   verily
I swear, 'tis better to be lowly born
And range with humble livers in content,
Than to be perked up in a glistening grief
And wear a golden sorrow."

SHAKSPERE.

ON Tuesday the 17th day of June 1567, Queen Mary found herself once more, and for the last time, journeying towards Lochleven Castle; but on this occasion it was under circumstances widely and painfully differing from those which had characterised her previous visits. Hitherto it had been to her a place of pleasant and welcome retreat, where, in her favourite pastime of hawking, and surrounded by her gay Court, she could for a time lay aside the harassing cares of State and forget the still more depressing personal anxieties which were gathering so thickly around her. Now it formed the "prison house" specially assigned to her by the Secret Council of the confederate Lords as "ane rowme maist convenient" for her detention, beyond the risk alike of rescue or escape. The warrant for her committal, which was signed late in the evening of Monday 16th June, by the Earls of Morton, Athol, Glencairn, and Mar, and by Lords Sempil, Ochiltree, and Graham, was in the following terms :—

"Ordanis, commandis, and chargeis Patrick Lord Lindsay

of the Byers, William Lord Ruthven, and Sir William Douglas of Lochleven, to pass and convoy Her Majesty to the said place of Lochleven, and the said laird to ressaive her thairin and thair thay and every ane of them to keep Her Majesty surelie within the said place."

It would indeed be difficult to realise the feelings with which the illustrious but unhappy captive must have viewed the Castle, as it met her gaze in the early dawn of the summer morning as she and her armed escort, at the close of their long weary midnight ride from Holyrood, rapidly rounded the western base of Benarty Hill, and swept down towards the margin of the lake. She was a woman of an intensely sensitive nature, and her thoughts and feelings must have been bitter and humiliating in the extreme, unless, indeed, the dreadful experiences of the past few days had rendered her, as they well might, utterly blind to all that was transpiring around her, and indifferent as to what further calamities fate might still have in store for her. Scarcely four months had yet elapsed since she had heard, amid the silence of midnight, the echoes of Holyrood resound to the roar of the explosion which hurled her unworthy husband to his last account; and in that interval, short as it was, she had been impelled to become the wife of the man who had acted as principal in her husband's assassination, and, as the immediate and natural result of that disastrous and unholy union, she had found herself face to face with her outraged subjects in open and armed revolt against her. The brief encounter on Carberry Hill, only two days previously, had been brought to a bloodless issue at the last moment by her separation from the unscrupulous villain for whom she had sacrificed so much, and by the bitter humiliation of her own personal surrender into the hands of her hostile nobles; and within the last few hours she had been subjected to the degradation of being led captive through the streets of her capital, amid the taunts and revilings of a ribald soldiery, and of a still more ribald populace—taunts and revilings of so base a character that the bare recollection of them was sufficient to cause her to shudder with horror. Whatever may have been her thoughts and feelings in the course of her midnight ride, it was certainly not a time favourable for the indulgence in bitter retrospect or vain sentimental regret. She was in the hands of Lord Lindsay and Lord Ruthven, both of them rude, unscrupulous and intensely practical men, to whom it had become a matter not merely of duty, but of direct personal safety, to see that their captive was securely immured within the sturdy keep which stood out before them in all its strength and isolation. Both of them had taken a prominent part in "the troubles" of the period, and both had a few months before actively aided in the cowardly assassination of Rizzio—Ruthven's father, indeed, with characteristic impetuosity having in the very presence of the Queen herself struck with his dagger the first blow at the doomed Secretary. Lord Lindsay, too, could scarcely fail to remember the bitter personal threat which the Queen in her frenzy had permitted herself to use towards him on Carberry Hill, only two days previously, when, in presence of the other confederate Lords, she laid her hand in his and uttered these pregnant words, "by the hand which is now in yours, I'll have your head for this." Certainly the Secret Council could not have selected men better suited for conducting the Queen to her place of imprisonment; and, with such extreme zeal did they discharge that undignified duty, that they barely extended towards her the ordinary consideration and courtesy which common humanity required. On the contrary they, under a fear that a rescue

might be attempted in the course of the journey, urged their
horses to their utmost speed, regardless of the fact that the
Queen was so wretchedly mounted, that one of their number
had continually to prick up her jaded steed in order to compel
it to keep pace with the rest of the band.

On reaching the Castle Island, accompanied by Lindsay
and Ruthven, the Queen was received by Sir William Douglas,
who had preceded her on her journey, in order to make the
requisite preparations for her arrival. Sir William was accompanied by his brother Robert, to whom reference has already
been made, and by George, his youngest brother, a young man
of about twenty-two or twenty-four years of age, whose subsequent association with the Queen was fated to influence powerfully the future lives of both. Immediately on reaching the Castle
the captive was conducted to the rooms which had been assigned
for her occupancy. If she anticipated that these would be the
regal apartments which she had so frequently occupied before,
and which she had herself fitted up with a view to her own personal comfort, and adorned in a manner suited to her refined
and cultivated tastes, she was doomed to disappointment, for
the rooms to which she was conducted were situated on the
ground floor—probably either the principal rooms in the range
east of the gateway, or, more probably still, those in the little
round tower already referred to; and, instead of these being
specially prepared for her use, they were furnished simply with
furniture belonging to the Laird of Lochleven, and little or no
effort had been made to lessen their repulsiveness and discom-
fort. When we consider the painful experiences and prolonged
excitement, and fatigue both of mind and body, through which
the Queen had just passed, it is not surprising to learn that on
her arrival at the Castle she was thoroughly prostrated by a

serious and alarming illness, and that for upwards of a fortnight she was obliged to be kept in strict and entire seclusion, unable to take any nourishment, and seeing no one but her own immediate personal attendants. These consisted of two of her bed-chamber women—Maria Courcelles and Jane Kennedy, who had alone been allowed to accompany her in her journey from Holyrood, and who, along with her own private surgeon, remained with her for the whole duration of her imprisonment in the Castle.

The illness of the Queen on her first arrival seems to have been of a very serious character, and for some time it was feared that it might even terminate fatally, but her wonderful energy of spirit, combined with the natural vigour of her constitution, carried her through this crisis of her life, as it carried her through many a past and many a future trial. On Tuesday the 1st of July, or exactly a fortnight after her long weary midnight ride from Holyrood, she was able to hold an interview with Sir Robert Melville, who was for some years in her service, and whom she had, early in the preceding month, sent on a special embassy to Queen Elizabeth to explain and excuse her marriage to Bothwell, and to endeavour to conciliate the English Court. Melville's visit was not of a disinterested character ; on the contrary, it covered an important diplomatic design, and if it had not done so, it would certainly have been prohibited by the confederate Lords. Their prominent desire at this time was to induce their captive to abdicate, and to establish a regency on behalf of her infant son and successor, then under the guardianship of the Earl of Mar in Stirling Castle—the contemplated Regent being Moray himself ; and knowing how much she relied on Melville's judgment and counsel, they selected him as her first visitor, and sent him to Lochleven Castle for the express purpose of persuading her to sign the formal abdication and letters of regency which they proposed shortly to lay before her. In order to add additional weight to Melville's advice, by making it appear that he was acting solely in her interests, and was therefore a person regarded with distrust and suspicion by the nobles, Lords Lindsay and Ruthven, along with Sir William Douglas, insisted on being present at this interview; and probably on this account, as well as owing to the continued weakness and prostration of the Queen, little or no progress was apparently made in the negotiation. Accordingly Melville is sent on a second mission to the Castle eight days afterwards, and on this occasion he is allowed for the first time to see the captive alone; but again it seems clear that no definite result was arrived at, although no doubt Melville broached the unpalatable subject of the proposed abdication and regency. A third and more protracted visit from Melville is therefore found necessary, and on this occasion the discussion is of a much more direct and practical character than it had been in the two previous interviews. Acting on the instructions of the confederate Lords, as well as from a desire, which no doubt was genuine and sincere on his own part, to secure the safety of his royal mistress, Melville urged her very strongly to accede to the wishes of the nobles, and to sign the abdication; and he strengthened this unpalatable counsel by pointing out to her that while her signature might lead to her regaining her liberty, it could not prejudice her interests or fetter her future action, seeing that it had been obtained under compulsion—an argument which was specially calculated to recommend itself to a person of Queen Mary's subtle nature.

At this third interview Melville entered upon even a more delicate and unpleasant subject of discussion, for we find that he urged her in the strongest possible terms to relinquish at once and for ever all connection with her bloody and unscrupulous husband Bothwell. In urging this Melville was no doubt also carrying out the instructions he had received from the nobles—instructions which in the circumstances he might have experienced some difficulty in giving effect to, had not she herself afforded him a favourable opportunity by soliciting him to forward to Bothwell a letter which she had in anticipation prepared. It is clear that at this time she still retained a tender feeling for the base and unworthy ruffian who had been the evil genius of her life and the cause of her ruin, for she positively refused to listen to the judicious counsel which Melville urged so strongly upon her ; and one of the chief reasons she gave for her refusal was that she believed herself to be with child to Bothwell, and feared that a divorce from him might be prejudicial to the interests of her unborn child by raising a doubt as to its legitimacy. If she was unyielding to Melville he was equally unyielding to her, for he positively refused to accept of her letter to Bothwell ; and at length, provoked at his stubborn refusal, she indignantly threw the letter into the fire.

This interview must have taken place between the 16th and the 18th days of July, and apparently its purport had been sufficiently satisfactory in the eyes of the Council to justify them in preparing the necessary documents, and, on the 24th day of July, the solitude of her imprisonment was again broken by a visit from Lindsay, Ruthven, and Melville, bearing the Abdication and Letters of Regency for her signature. During the interval between this date and the date of Melville's previous visit, the Queen had again been dangerously ill, and her illness had, according to an incidental statement by Nau, resulted in a miscarriage. There seems to be no reason to doubt the truth of this statement, and it is one of not a little importance, as it entirely refutes the deliberate allegation of some of the French biographers of the Queen, that she, while in Lochleven Castle, bore a daughter to Bothwell, who, in after life, became a nun in the convent of Soissons.

This illness had left the Queen in a state of extreme weakness and prostration, and she was in consequence confined to bed when she was waited upon by her visitors. The trying and painful scene which took place at the signing of the Abdication and Letters of Regency must have been of a character most unsuited for a sick chamber. Melville was first allowed to see the Queen alone, and he used every argument his ingenuity could suggest to induce her to comply with the demands of the confederate Lords; and, in order to strengthen still further the special argument which he had urged on the previous occasion, he dramatically produced from the scabbard of his sword, where he said he had carried it in secret at the very risk of his life, a private letter to the Queen from Throgmorton, the English ambassador, in which he, by the express authority of his mistress, Queen Elizabeth, urged her, as Melville had already done, to secure her personal safety and freedom by signing the deeds, and on her regaining her liberty she would be quite entitled to repudiate them on the ground that they were not her voluntary act. Melville also conveyed messages of similar effect from the Queen's personal adherents, the Earl of Athole, Lord Lethington, and the Laird of Tullibardine; and, in token of the veracity of these messages he handed to her from Athole a turquoise which the Earl had previously received from her, and from Lord Lethington a small oval ornament of gold, enamelled with a representation of Æsop's fable of the mouse liberating the lion, which also had been a gift from her, while Tullibardine committed to Melville a password which her Majesty and he had previously agreed upon between themselves. These persuasions seem to have been of no avail, or, at all events the Queen was too politic to show, even to Melville, any symptoms of acquiescence in the advice he had tendered to her; and he, apparently still without any definite assurance as to the course she meant to follow, at length ushered into the Queen's bed-chamber Lindsay and Ruthven, along with the two Notaries who had accompanied them from Edinburgh for the purpose of formally authenticating her subscription. According to Sir James Melville's "Memoir," founded on information received directly from his brother Robert, the Queen refused to follow the advice urged upon her, "but when she heard that the Lord Lindsay was at the New House, and was upon a boisting humour, she yielded to the necessitie of the time, and showed my brother that she wald not stryve with them, seeing it could do her na harm when she was at liberty."

Lindsay and Ruthven, immediately on entering the Queen's apartment, ordered the two female attendants to retire, and then Lindsay, irritated at the delay which had already taken place, announced, with characteristic audacity and rudeness, the purport of their visit, and peremptorily requested the Queen to read the documents to which they were instructed to obtain her signature. With much dignity of manner she plainly and deliberately refused to do so, and stated that her conscience would not permit her to grant any documents of such a nature. Lindsay's rage at her dignified and persistent refusal overmastered him to such an extent that he rudely ordered her to rise from her bed, as in the event of her refusal, his orders were to take her to a place where "he would give a good account of her," pointing out to her in coarse and brutal terms that her refusal would only compel them, however unwilling they might be, to put her to death. Worn out by her bodily weakness, and by the rude and violent persistency of Lindsay, she was compelled to listen to the deeds as these were read aloud by the Notaries, and she then signed them, protesting, at the same time, that her signature was no evidence of her consent, and calling those present to witness that she would repudiate the documents the moment she regained her liberty. This bold announcement irritated Lindsay still more, and extorted from him the significant rejoinder that the resolution she had expressed would only entail upon them the necessity of taking special care that she never had the power to carry out her intention.

This exciting interview, in the Queen's weak condition, threw her into a state of great agitation and distress, not unmixed with fear and anxiety, as to the course which her persecutors might next resort to. Lindsay's significant threat, in particular, seems to have given rise to the belief that she was about to be removed from Lochleven, and committed to some place of more secure detention, where she would be entirely beyond the reach of her friends and adherents, and where even her death might be encompassed with no possibility of its ever being known or detected. Melville, in a private interview immediately afterwards, endeavoured by every means in his power to allay the agitation and fears of his mistress, and among other soothing and encouraging expressions he suggested the possibility of her escape from Lochleven, and indicated to her that she would find in George Douglas, the youngest brother of her custodian, one who was anything but unfriendly to her, as he had, in an interview with him in the garden, showed much distress at the indignity with which she had been treated. In her usual impulsive manner she at once sent a message by Melville to

George Douglas, claiming his protection, and urging him to intercede with his brother Sir William, to prevent her from being removed to any other place of imprisonment. George Douglas was at this time a young man of about twenty-four years of age, and, as the Queen's youth and beauty and misfortunes had already awakened in his heart that chivalrous devotion which afterwards led him to peril his whole future prospects, and his life itself for her sake, it is not surprising that he replied to his Sovereign's message in person by accompanying Melville at once to her apartment. This appears to have been the first confidential interview between the Queen and George Douglas, for hitherto she had, at the instigation of Lord Ruthven, regarded him as a personal enemy, and as one whose sympathies were entirely with the confederate Lords. The interview was on both sides perfectly satisfactory, and she having voluntarily assured George Douglas that the effect of her liberation would neither be injurious to his half-brother Moray, nor to his brother Sir William Douglas, or any member of his household, he pledged himself to do the utmost he possibly could to aid in reinstating her in her former regal position and influence.

Sir William Douglas, although the real custodian of the Queen, was not present when the Abdication was signed, and there is every reason to surmise that his absence was deliberate and intentional ; at all events it was made the excuse for a subsequent and superfluous formality on his part, which was clearly intended to strengthen the position of the confederate Lords, by affording additional evidence of the abdication having been a purely voluntary act. Accordingly, on the day after the painful and trying scene above narrated, Sir William, accompanied by two Notaries, appeared before the Queen, and, under a pretended fear lest he might be held responsible for the previous day's transactions, he requested, says the written Protest, "to know how, in his absence, Her Majesty had demitted the Crown, and he now wished to learn whether the act had been done of her own will and free consent. Thereupon the Queen homologated the act and declared that she had not been compelled; and Douglas protests that hereafter she should not be held to have been a captive, and under constraint at the doing thereof." How far the Queen expressed either homologation or concurrence may well be doubted; the probability rather is that she regarded Sir William's specious proceedings with indifference, and allowed them to pass without comment or remark, for, to her acute intellect, it must have been clearly apparent that the alleged homologation was open to precisely the same objection as the abdication itself, the circumstances attending the execution of the one being equally applicable to the execution of the other.

Among the reasons urged to induce the Queen to sign the abdication, she must have been led to believe that pending her release, her imprisonment would be rendered less rigorous and irksome than it had hitherto been, and in fulfilment of this promise she was shortly removed from the rooms to which she had been consigned on her first arrival at the Castle, and which she had now occupied for nearly a month, and taken to other apartments in what Nau calls "the gloomy tower," meaning undoubtedly the principal keep. Apparently this change was not altogether to the Queen's satisfaction, probably for the simple reason that it placed her much more directly under the surveillance of Sir William Douglas and his household, and it was accomplished only after great altercation on both sides. If any modification in her imprisonment was hoped for, that hope was doomed to disappointment, for she continued to be as strictly

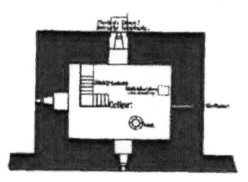

Plan of Ground Floor.

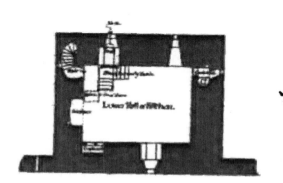

Plan of First Floor.

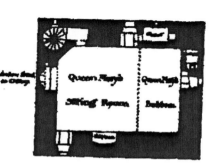

Plan of Third Floor.

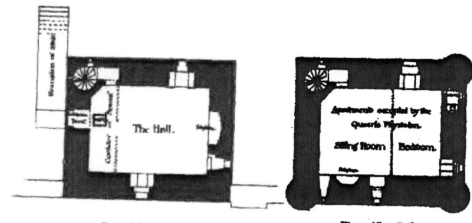

Plan of Second Floor.

Plan of fourth floor.

PLANS OF KEEP.

Plate IV.

Page 57

guarded in her new quarters as she had been in the rooms which she occupied at first—a daughter and a niece of Sir William Douglas being actually appointed to sleep in the Queen's bed-chamber in order that her every movement both by night and day might be closely watched.

According to the contemporary details now supplied by Nau's "Memorial," the rooms at this period assigned to Queen Mary were clearly those forming the third floor of the square tower—the first floor immediately above the dungeon flat being occupied as the kitchen, while the second floor immediately above the kitchen formed the dining-hall or principal apartment of the Castle. Into this hall led the only doorway giving access from the courtyard to the interior of the tower, and there are still to be seen in the existing walls the holes in which rested the beams supporting a partition which separated the hall from the entrance doorway, and thus formed a long narrow lobby or corridor, stretching along the whole breadth of the tower. This corridor secured the privacy of the hall, as it afforded a means by which access could be had from the entrance doorway to the spiral staircase leading to the rooms above, without passing through the dining-hall. The first floor above the hall contained the rooms assigned for the Queen's use, and it appears to have been sub-divided into a sitting room on the east side, and one sleeping apartment, if not two, on the west side. On this floor, as well as in the floor above, which seems to have been sub-divided in a similar manner, there was no corridor, the entrance from the spiral stair in both entering directly into the sitting room, and the sleeping apartments beyond could only be reached by traversing the sitting rooms. In the recess of one of the windows of the Queen's sitting room looking to the south, there is constructed in the thickness of the wall a small but very interesting closet, and in the recess of the east window of the same room, there are indications as if it had been fitted up as a small oratory or place of devotion. The Queen's surgeon occupied the floor immediately above her apartments. It is necessary thus minutely to indicate these rooms, as hitherto there has been an almost universal but mistaken belief that she was imprisoned, during the whole time she was in Lochleven Castle, in the small south-east tower to which special reference has already been made; and before leaving this interesting subject, it may not be out of place to indicate to those who are inclined to test the truth of Nau's statement, by a critical examination of the tower itself, that the rooms referred to form the only portion of the tower in which the plaster still adheres to the walls, showing clearly that they had undergone a thorough renovation at, comparatively speaking, a recent period, and it is not unreasonable to conjecture that they may have been prepared specially for the Queen's use during the first month of her imprisonment, while she was temporarily occupying the rooms to which she was first consigned.

The signing of the Abdication and Letters of Regency by the Queen must have been a great relief to the minds of the confederate Lords, and they lost not a moment in giving effect to them by establishing the Regency, providing for their own personal immunity from their late acts of treason, and making arrangements for the immediate coronation of the infant Prince; and Moray, who had judiciously betaken himself to France immediately after Darnley's assassination, was urgently recalled to this country. The coronation of the infant sovereign, James VI., took place on the 27th of July, or within three days after the date of his mother's signature to the abdication.

On this occasion Sir William Douglas, in his satisfaction at seeing his half-brother Moray vested in the Regency, appears to have allowed his zeal for the new regime to overcome his sense of the consideration due to his unfortunate but distinguished captive, for we are told that he celebrated that event by lighting bonfires and firing all the available pieces of ordnance on the Castle walls, and otherwise indulging in boisterous demonstrations of rejoicing. These could not fail to be distasteful and painful to the Queen. Weakened in health and crushed by the calamities thickly gathering around her, she had evidently not been informed of what was transpiring outside the walls of her room, for when, startled by the noise and commotion, she enquired as to the cause of the uproar, she was informed that it was in celebration of the coronation of her infant son as her successor. This unpalatable explanation was conveyed to her by Sir William Douglas himself, and in course of the painful interview which ensued between the Queen and him in her apartment, the unhappy captive, overwhelmed by a sense of her utter helplessness, and realising probably for the first time how little she had to expect from the tender mercies of her enemies, in a paroxysm of grief threw herself upon her knees in the middle of her chamber near the table and wept long and bitterly

CHAPTER V.

QUEEN MARY'S IMPRISONMENT—*continued.*

Now blooms the lily by the bank,
  The primrose down the brae ;
The hawthorn's budding in the glen,
  And milk-white is the slae :
The meanest hind in fair Scotland
  May rove their sweets amang ;
But I, the Queen of a' Scotland,
  Maun lie in prison strang.
                                        BURNS.

THE extreme haste with which the Council proceeded to carry into effect the Queen's abdication, coupled with the fact that instead of her imprisonment being rendered less severe it was actually made more rigorous and strict, seems to have had the effect of enabling her more thoroughly to realise her true position and prospects. She still clung to the hope, however, that the return of her illegitimate brother the Earl of Moray from France, would lead to her immediate release and her ultimate re-establishment in her former regal position and power. Alike from his influential rank and distinguished ability he was undoubtedly the prominent man of the period; and as his intercourse with the Queen had always been of a most affectionate and fraternal character up to the time when Darnley became her accepted suitor, it was natural that she should look to him for that counsel and protection which she now so sorely needed. Accordingly the first instance in which she availed herself of the services of her new adherent George Douglas, was to send him to meet his half-brother Moray and advise with him as to the course which she wished him to pursue in the present important crisis in her affairs. Moray, with his characteristic forethought and cold calculating diplomacy, had taken care to dissociate himself from the confederate Lords in their recent revolt, and had remained in France until he heard of the Queen's incarceration in Lochleven Castle. So soon as he regarded the course of events as sufficiently advanced for his re-appearance on the scene, he at once returned to Scotland, and put himself into communication in the first instance with Queen Elizabeth and her advisers, and afterwards with the confederate Lords, who, in their whole dealings with Queen Mary, both before and since her imprisonment, were clearly acting the part of mere cat's-paw to Moray, and aiding him in carrying out the great object he then had in view—the securing of the regency during the long minority of the infant prince. Moray seems to have been in no haste to enter the presence of his captive sovereign and sister. On the contrary, his movements were of the most deliberate character, and it was only after she had heard of his arrival in Scotland, and while he was still delaying to seek an interview with her, that she sent George Douglas to inform him fully of the circumstances under which she had been compelled to sign the abdication, and to warn him on no account to accept the regency. Douglas' mission does not appear to have been a very successful one, for he failed to discover Moray's real sentiments and intentions towards his sister, and in regard to the regency, he received but a cold and indifferent reply.

Moray's first visit to the Queen at Lochleven Castle took

place on the evening of the 15th of August, nearly a fortnight
after his return from France.   He arrived about the supper hour
(7 o'clock), just as she was about to sit down at table.   The
Earls of Morton, Athole, and Lord Lindsay accompanied him,
and he, along with Morton and Athole, were at once ushered
into the royal presence.   His manner towards his sister was
studied, artificial and constrained, and he evidently wished to
avoid, if he possibly could, any approach towards private or
confidential conversation with her.   She, however, had too much
at stake to be easily thwarted in her desire for the private
interview which she had looked forward to with so much
anxiety for the last two months, and with some difficulty she
succeeded in inducing him to remain with her when his companions left the room ; and even this favour he conceded only
after formally asking and obtaining the consent of the others.
If she clung, as no doubt she must have clung, to the hope that
Moray, when relieved from the presence of Morton and Athole,
would relax in his manner towards her, and resume the cordial
and affectionate bearing which he had shown in brighter and
happier days, she must have experienced a cruel and bitter
disappointment, for, when they were alone, he still retained his
cold reserve, in spite of her frantic appeals and passionate tears.
When supper was served he even refused to sup with her,
although she specially requested him to do so ; and he would
have availed himself of the opportunity of quitting the apartment
while she supped had she not pointedly reminded him that in
former days he had not thought it beneath him to " give her the
napkin " at table.   After supper she again succeeded in compelling
him to accord to her a further private interview.   It commenced
in the garden attached to the Castle, where they sauntered
backwards and forwards for a considerable time, and afterwards

it was continued within doors until an hour after midnight. Still Moray continued cold and unfriendly, and instead of expressions of sympathy and kindness, he conducted himself towards her more like a "ghostly father" than a near and affectionate relative. The interview terminated without the slightest ray of hope or comfort being extended by Moray to his unfortunate sister. As the English ambassador puts it, Moray left her that night "in hope of nothing but God's mercy;" while Nau states that he left her without indicating whether he intended to act as her friend or not. Fain would the Queen, in her unhappiness and friendlessness, have induced Moray to remain with her for a day or two to advise more fully as to her affairs, but this was exactly what he wished above all things to avoid, and he positively refused, on the plea that it would expose him to the suspicion of his confederates. He saw her, however, once more the following morning, just before leaving the Castle. Again the subject of the previous night's discussion was introduced, and Moray, in a more gracious mood, or anxious, probably, to soothe her, and terminate as quickly as possible an ordeal which could not fail to be painfully embarrassing to him, permitted himself to express to her some vague words of consolation, and to assure her that he would secure the safety at least of her person, but as for her liberty, "it lay not in his power, nor was it good for her to seek it, nor presently to have it, in many respects." When the time for parting came she bade adieu to Morton and Athole with that queenly grace and dignity which she could so well assume, and which so well became her. "My Lords," she said, "you have had experience of my severity and of the end of it, I pray you also let me find that you have learned by me to make an end of yours or at least that you make it final." To Moray, in spite of his cold reserve towards her, she was kind and affectionate, throwing herself into his arms with a hysterical burst of weeping, and imploring him to carry her blessing to the infant prince, her son.   Moray, with pretentious consideration for her comfort, summoned before him Sir William Douglas and Lord Lindsay, and enjoined them in her presence to treat her with gentleness, and to allow her all the liberty that could be granted, and he and his companions then hastened to take their departure for Stirling.

At a very early period of the Queen's imprisonment, schemes for her release were entertained and discussed among her adherents, but the great obstacle which at that time prevented these from being carried into effect was undoubtedly not so much the difficulty of effecting her liberation, as of providing for her security and re-instatement in power after she was liberated. Strong as the Castle naturally was, there were available means by which a resolute and well organised band of from 50 to 100 men might at any time have seized it by surprise, and secured possession of its illustrious inmate, more especially while she had within the walls of the Castle so devoted an adherent as George Douglas, occupying a prominent, and no doubt influential position in the limited garrison by which it was protected. The fighting men within the Castle—according to a contemporary account—did not exceed fifteen or sixteen in number, and the insular position it occupied, although a formidable obstacle, could scarcely be regarded as an insurmountable one, so long as there were, at the fishing villages on the Forth, boats that could, in the course of three or four hours, have been easily transported in secret to the shores of the lake.

It is clear, that from the moment of the Queen's surrender at Carberry Hill, her supporters had become thoroughly and hopelessly disorganised; and although Bothwell, within a fortnight after her committal to Lochleven Castle, used strenuous means to organise a fresh effort on her behalf, its only result had been a disclosure to him of the painful fact that his power and influence were irretrievably gone, and that the only means by which he could save his miserable life were ignominious flight and perpetual exile. In fact the hopes of the Queen's best friends were, like the hopes of her worst enemies, centred exclusively in Moray as the only man who could satisfactorily solve the great State problem of the day, and his return to Scotland was at that time looked forward to with eagerness by both factions alike—by the Queen's adherents, in the confident hope that his judicious influence would bring about her immediate release and re-instatement in her former regal position and power, free from all the complications which arose from her connection with Bothwell; and by her opponents, in the equally confident hope that it would lead to the establishment of a long Regency, and the permanent exclusion of the Queen from interfering in the affairs of the kingdom. Moray's delay in returning from France had necessarily prolonged this interval of suspense, and in the meantime the disorganisation of the Queen's faction daily increased, until at length the final blow was struck by the establishment of the Regency, and still more by the prudent and highly politic course of action which Moray adopted from the moment of his accession to power. This had materially weakened the Queen's cause, as it had thrown those of the nobility who still supported her into a state of indecision, if not of positive dissension. At the same time there were still a few who were unwavering in their loyalty and devotion; and so soon as Moray's actings as Regent disclosed the fact that the liberation and re-instatement of the Queen formed no part of his policy, these proceeded

E

at once to organise themselves into a faction, and to devise
means for defeating Moray's ambitious and crooked schemes.
A bond to the following effect was accordingly entered into, not
only by the staunchest adherents of the Queen, but by some of
the other nobles who had recently been in league with Moray,
but who, disliking his predominance, were now prone to make
common cause with his opponents :—

"For, samelike as considering the Queen's Majestie our Sovereign
to be detainit in Lochleven in captivity, wherethrough the maist part
of her Grace's lieges cannot have free access to her hyness for doing
of their lawful business, and, by reason it becomes us of our duty to
'suit' her liberty and freedom, We, Earls, Lords, and Barons under
subscribed promise faithfully to make our exact diligence by all reasonable means to 'suit' her Majesty to be put to liberty and freedom,
upon such honest conditions as may stand with her Highness' honor,
the common weal of this hail nation, and security of the hail nobility
of the same, and with the security of the noblemen who presently have
her Majesty in keeping, wherethrough this, our native realm, may be
governed, ruled, and guided by her Majesty and her nobility, for the
common quietness, administration of justice, and weal of the country;
And, in case the noblemen who has her Majesty presently in their hands
refuse to put her to liberty upon sic reasonable means and conditions as
said is, in that case we shall employ ourselves, our kin and friends,
servants and partakers, our bodies and lives to put her Highness to liberty,
as said is, and also to concur to the punishment of the murder of the
King her Majesty's husband, and for sure preservation of the person
of the Prince, as we shall answer to God, and on our honors and credit,
and to this effect shall concur every ane with other at our utter power,
and gin any shall put at us, or any of us, for the doing of the causes
foresaid, in that case we promise faithfully to take 'efautel' part every
one with other under the pain of perjury and infamy, as we will

answer to God as said is.—In witness of the whilk we have subscribed thes presents with our hands at Dumbarton, this   day of

(*Signed,*) St Andrews; Argyle; Huntly; Arbroath; Galloway; Ross; Fleming; Herries; Skirling; Kilwinning; William Hamilton of Sanquhar, Knight."

These "signatories," according to Sir James Melville's "Memoirs," were only these of "the few that first band themselves together, and afterwards all of them that were malcontents or had any particular question, claim, or feud with any of the King's Lords, drew to their new confederates, hoping with time to win their intent against their adversary in case the faction might prevail." It is thus evident that the Queen's faction at the best was not very strong either in numbers or in unanimity and cohesiveness of principle.

In such circumstances it must have been clear to the Queen's adherents that although there were means by which they could at almost any moment have effected her liberation, nothing but hopeless and irretrievable disaster could result from the attainment of that object if due provision was not first made for the inevitable sequel to that event—the necessity for her meeting in open field the organised forces of her opponents, and fighting her way through them back to the throne of her fathers from which she had been expelled. To provide for this necessity, as well as to effect the Queen's liberation, therefore formed the difficult double problem of which the chivalrous and devoted George Douglas had taken the solution in hand, and, in his efforts to solve it, he was fortunate in finding an able and indefatigable coadjutor in John Beton, the brother of the Archbishop of Glasgow, and one of the Queen's staunchest adherents. Impelled by a disinterested feeling of the truest loyalty and devotion, Beton, from the moment of her incarceration within the Castle, had never ceased to hover around her prison in the hope of getting conveyed to her some expression of his continued fidelity to her cause, and of receiving in reply an indication of any service he could render to her; and no doubt the Queen would lose not a moment after her first interview with George Douglas in putting her new adherent into confidential communication with that tried and faithful follower. It was probably by this means that Beton received the letters which, at an early period of her imprisonment she addressed to her powerful friends and relatives in France, informing them of her position and imploring their aid, and which ultimately reached their destination through Beton's services. The following touching letter, addressed by her at this period to the Queen of France, was one of the letters so forwarded, and it shows that the want of organisation among her supporters formed at that time the real weakness of her cause and the true reason for no immediate effort being made for her liberation :—

"LOCHLEVEN (*undated*).

„ MADAM,—I write to you at the same time as to the King, your son, and by the same bearer, to beseech you both to have pity upon me. I am now fully convinced that it is by force alone I can be delivered. If you send never so few troops to countenance the matter, I am certain great numbers of my subjects will rise to join them, but without that they are overawed by the force of the rebels, and dare attempt nothing of themselves. The miseries I endure are more than I once believed it was in the power of human sufferance to sustain and live. Give credit to this messenger, who can tell you all. I have no opportunity to write, but while my jailors are at dinner. Have compassion, I conjure you, on my wretched condition, and may God pour on you all the blessings you can desire—Your ever dutiful, though most wretched and afflicted daughter,   M. R."

"From my Prison, to Madam, the Queen of France,
              my Mother-in-law."

Through Beton George Douglas was also put into confidential communication with other supporters of the Queen, who were then devoting themselves to her interests—Lord Seton, one of the oldest and most staunch and loyal of all her friends, and John Sempil, the husband of Mary Livingston, one of the "four Maries." In regard to Lord Seton, Beton anticipated that difficulties might arise, owing to a deadly feud which had long existed between the Setons and the Douglasses, and which rendered it impossible to persuade a Douglas of the fidelity of a Seton, or a Seton to trust to the constancy of a Douglas. In anticipating this difficulty, Beton seems to have underestimated the overpowering influence of the common cause which both Seton and Douglas had so much at heart, for, in their devotion to their Sovereign, and their single hearted zeal for her restoration, their personal differences were at once laid aside, and they became the firmest and most steadfast associates.

The earliest project for the Queen's liberation, according to a contemporary writing, was, unlike the later attempts, of a somewhat bold and hazardous nature, involving the taking possession of the large boat used for transporting coals and other heavy goods, which is stated to have been capable of accommodating from sixty to eighty men, and manning it with a chosen number of adherents, who were to assault the Castle by night, and, assisted by George Douglas and some of his confederates from within, force their way into the tower where the Queen was imprisoned, and carry her off. This plot does not appear to have assumed a very definite shape, owing probably to the fact already adverted to, that the time for its accomplishment had not yet arrived, and it was frustrated at the outset by Will Drysdale, the principal officer of the garrison in the Castle, whom George Douglas seems to have relied on for aid in the enterprise. Drysdale conveyed to his master, Sir William Douglas, a vague and indefinite suggestion that the large boat should be properly secured, without apparently disclosing any particulars of the contemplated scheme, and acting on this hint, Sir William laid up the boat on shore, and fastened it securely with chains, so that it could not be launched without the use of very considerable force.

The failure of this scheme seems to have occasioned much disappointment, and a period of comparative inactivity ensued, while the autumn and winter months dragged on their long weary course. To relieve the monotony of her life the captive had recourse to her favourite occupation of needle work, and among the articles she received from time to time from Holyrood were many of the requisites for embroidery, an art in which she specially excelled. Many exquisite specimens of her skilful and tasteful execution of this art are yet to be seen in Scotland, and one of the most interesting of these is a folding screen now at Dalmahoy House, the tapestry on which is believed to be the identical work on which she was engaged during her residence in the Castle, and which she left behind her in an unfinished state at the time of her escape. This screen, according to Miss Strickland, affords in itself evidence that this belief is well founded, as it actually "depicts the story of her wrongs, and the relentless malice of her powerful foe." At this period also she seems to have become more patient and resigned under her irksome confinement, for, to use the words of a contemporary writer, she, in her intercourse with those with whom she was brought in contact, "so conducted herself as to give the impression that she submitted both her fortunes and herself entirely to their pleasure." Much of her time and thought was devoted to religious duties and exercises, and by her gentleness and

QUEEN MARY'S ROOM.

(restored)

Plate V

ascination she completely secured the pity and sympathy, not only of old Lady Douglas—but even of Sir William Douglas and his wife, as well as of their daughter and niece, to whom had been assigned the ignominious duty of acting as spies on her movements. Sir William Douglas' wife, in particular, was of material aid in not only secretly furnishing her with means by which she could write to her friends, but even in undertaking to forward her letters to their destination.

During this period of inaction and repose Moray visited the Queen in her captivity at least once, and apparently oftener. In the Exchequer Records there is an entry under date 23rd October 1567, to the following effect :—"To my Lord Regent's grace to give the Queen's Majesty at Lochleven, £100," and at the close of the short Parliament in December 1567, Moray again ventured into the presence of his sister. His visit on this occasion was one of marked formality and characterised by considerable pomp, as he was accompanied by the Earl of Morton, and several other leading noblemen of the day. Among these was Sir James Balfour, formerly a creature of Bothwell's, and one of the prime movers in Darnley's assassination, to whom had been entrusted the keeping of Edinburgh Castle, in the interest of the Queen, but who had been bribed by Moray to betray his trust, and to surrender the Castle and deliver up the jewels and other private property and papers which the Queen and Bothwell had left in his hands. The object of this visit history affords to us no means of ascertaining ; but, being of a formal and imposing character, it can scarcely be doubted that the audience with the Queen took place not in the limited space of her private sitting-room, but either in the more spacious presence-chamber in the courtyard or in the dining-hall in the square tower. Wherever it was held it must have proved an unpleasant ordeal for all the nobles, and especially so for Moray, who could scarcely fail to contrast the Queen's manner towards him on this occasion with that which characterised her reception of him when he first visited her in her captivity. Then she had clung to him with all the trustfulness of a helpless and persecuted sister, now she asserted herself as an outraged monarch and as a generous benefactress whose sisterly trust and leniency towards him had been basely perverted into means to accomplish her ruin.

The very opening of the interview was of a somewhat ominous character, and formed a fitting prelude to what was to follow. The day on which the visit took place was unusually quiet and still, but at the very instant when Moray and his companions were entering the Queen's presence a sudden and unexpected gust of wind broke upon the Castle and violently burst open the lattice windows of the room in which they were assembled. Every one was startled at the occurrence, and the Queen at once turned it to effective account by pointedly and incisively remarking that the sudden and violent commotion " must of necessity be for some arch traitor," and the steadfast look which she fixed on Sir James Balfour compelled him to accept the observation as specially applicable to himself, and reddening excessively he retired behind the backs of the people who had accompanied the nobles. Having thus summarily disposed of Balfour, she at once turned to her brother Moray, and literally overwhelmed him with a torrent of bitter reproaches. She reminded him of the sisterly affection with which she had all along regarded him, of the unlimited trust she had always reposed in him, of the leniency with which she had forgiven his repeated acts of disloyalty towards her, and of the many substantial marks of her favour of which he had been the recipient.

She also enumerated the just and reasonable demands which she had made to him, not for her liberty, but for what she valued far more highly, an opportunity of appearing before the Council and justifying herself against the vile accusations which had been brought against her—demands which he had always refused to give effect to—and she upbraided him for the injustice and baseness with which he had acted towards her in every particular and constituted himself as her mortal and sworn enemy. With firm decisiveness of manner she declined to hold further intercourse with him on any occasion whatever, saying she would rather wear out her life in perpetual imprisonment than accept of her freedom at his hands, and she concluded with a fervent hope that the just God, the avenger of the oppressed, would free her to his disgrace, damage, and ruin. The Earl of Morton alone seems to have ventured on the *rôle* of peace-maker, and he spoke very courteously to her Majesty and expressed his desire to do anything in his power for her. The storm, however, was too great to be allayed by Morton's feeble though well meant words, and she indignantly and proudly proceeded to leave the apartment. In the act of doing so she stopped for an instant in front of Moray, and, seizing hold of his hand, she openly and in presence of them all, protested that, cost what it might, sooner or later he should repent his perfidy to her.

The feelings with which Moray listened to this torrent of only too well-founded accusation and reproach may be more easily imagined than described, and before leaving the Castle he displayed the extent of his irritation and annoyance by entering upon an angry altercation with his half-brother George Douglas, whom he peremptorily ordered to leave the Castle and never again to enter it, or if he did so he would have him hanged. The readiness with which Moray selected him as the scapegoat for the indignity which in the very sight of all his principal confederates he had been called upon to bear, evidently arose from his strong conviction that it was from him alone that the Queen could have received the full and accurate information as to all his recent movements, which had added so much to the telling force of the accusations and complaints levelled against him.   Nor is this conviction on Moray's part a matter for surprise, for George Douglas's devotion to the Queen had by this time attracted not a little public notice, and had even been made the subject of remark in one of the contemporary gossiping letters which were continually passing between Sir William Drury and Queen Elizabeth's powerful minister Cecil.

Sir William Douglas, owing probably to the interposition of his mother, Lady Douglas, who was tenderly attached to her youngest son, or more probably still, to his regarding Moray's words as merely the expression of the temporary irritation resulting from the trying and humiliating ordeal to which he had been subjected, does not appear to have strictly carried out the Regent's order for his brother's expulsion, and still allowed him to remain in dangerous proximity to the fair and interesting captive.   It would even appear that Moray himself must shortly afterwards have modified, if he did not altogether abandon, his suspicions, for we find that George Douglas, when sent by the Queen on a future mission to Moray, was actually entrusted by Moray with the delivery of his reply to the Queen's communication.   No sooner, however, had Douglas set out on his return journey than Moray's former suspicions were by some cause aroused anew and in a more intensified form, and he immediately dispatched a messenger in hot haste to Sir William Douglas at Lochleven forbidding the Laird to allow his brother to enter the Castle.   George Douglas by some means discovered that such a messenger had been dispatched, but he contrived to outstrip him and reached the Castle before him.

George Douglas now seems to have realised the fact that he could no longer remain within the Castle walls without entailing disastrous results not merely on himself and his mother and brother, but even on her whose liberty he was heart and soul bent on securing. In his brief and hurried interview with the Queen—for he knew that Moray's messenger was close at his heels—he explained to her what had occurred, bade her a last farewell, and acquainted her fully of the details of a scheme which was then contemplated for her liberation, and the part which she herself would be expected to bear in it. He also urged her to endeavour by every means in her power to secure the aid of Willie Douglas, a clever and intelligent youth of sixteen years of age, who had charge of the boats at the Castle, as his assistance was of special importance in the successful carrying out of their scheme, seeing that it was only through him that a continual means of communication could be provided It was in all likelihood at this interview that the Queen took out one of the ear-rings she usually wore—a pearl drop shaped like a pear—and gave it to Douglas, with instructions to return it to her as a signal whenever their plans for her escape were fully matured. He also had entrusted to him on this occasion a letter hurriedly written by the Queen to her staunch and loyal friend and adherent Lord Seton. This letter must have been of the briefest possible character, for it was written under great difficulties. Paper and ink had always been rigidly withheld from her, and she was therefore compelled to make her own ink for the occasion with the soot in the chimney, and she is even alleged to have written her communication on her handkerchief as a substitute for paper. In bidding adieu to

the Queen, Douglas again fervently renewed his oath that he
would faithfully render to her all the loyalty and fidelity of
a good subject, and protested that he would continue to do
so until death.

Scarcely had this hurried and exciting interview closed when
George Douglas was met by his brother Sir William as he was
leaving the Queen's apartments, and told of Moray's prohibition,
and commanded peremptorily to leave the Castle at once, and
never again to enter it or come near it. An unseemly altercation
unhappily occurred between the two brothers, for George, offended
at the treatment which he was receiving, and feeling that further
concealment was now useless, angrily upbraided his brother
for the unworthy part he was acting. His mother, too, was
in deep distress at her son's expulsion, but she felt that his
continued presence in the Castle was for many reasons un-
desirable for himself, and would only entail ruin on her eldest
son and their whole house. So bitter and hostile was the
feeling between the two brothers, that, even afterwards, when
time must have somewhat cooled Sir William's anger, he ordered
a cannon shot to be fired at his brother from the Castle in
consequence of his having, for the purpose of signalling
to the Queen, recklessly approached too near the Island by
riding his horse as far as he could into the waters of the loch.
No doubt the not unfriendly gunner, while complying with his
master's orders, would, out of consideration for George Douglas,
send the shot at a safe distance over-head, but not the less it must
have been to him a somewhat startling proof of his brother's
determination to allow no further tampering with the grave
trust and responsibility imposed upon him. Several years ago
a cannon ball of antique character, composed of a com-
bination of metal and stone, between four and five pounds in

weight, was found embedded in the shore near Roy's Folly at the back of the old churchyard of Kinross. This ball is still preserved by Mr David Marshall, Kinross; and who knows but it may form the veritable expression of fraternal love and regard with which Sir William Douglas on this occasion so startled his younger brother. Far-fetched as this suggestion may seem, there is at all events this to be said in support of it, that the line of fire from the Castle to the place where the ball was found crosses the very spot which, by any one familiar with the loch, as George Douglas must have been from boyhood upwards, would be selected as the nearest and most favourable for attracting the attention of any one walking in the Castle garden.

This incident naturally tended still further to embitter the feelings of the brothers towards each other, and from this time George Douglas threw aside all attempts to conceal his devotion to the cause of the Queen, and, lurking in the vicinity of Lochleven, he became the enthusiastic and energetic leader and originator of all the schemes that were devised for her escape. In these schemes it is evident that he aimed at effecting his purpose less by force than by stratagem. For this he had no doubt weighty reasons, not the least of which would be his natural reluctance to expose the Queen, or even his brother and the members of his household to the risk of bodily injury during the course of an open and violent attack upon the Castle. This explains the importance which he attached to Willie Douglas's services, and no doubt the Queen, acting on his suggestion, would lose not a moment in bringing her irresistible fascination to bear upon the lad, with the view of securing his thorough and heartfelt devotion to her cause. Willie was a clever, intelligent, and superior youth of somewhat mysterious parentage, having been found deposited on the Island as a mere infant, and for this reason he was generally familiarly styled "The Foundling." He was brought up in Sir William Douglas's household, and, as he bore Sir William's name, it has been conjectured that he was an illegitimate son of his patron. He seems to have been a general favourite in the Castle, and Sir William, who acted towards him in a kind and interested way, had given him an excellent and even a refined education.

In consequence, probably, of the severity of the winter, and the impossibility of following up by active operations in the field the advantage to be gained by the Queen's liberation, the projects of George Douglas and his companions were allowed to lie in abeyance till the return of spring, and in the interval, the freedom from renewed attempts at escape may have tended to allay any suspicions that had been aroused by the abortive effort of the previous autumn. In February, too, the Queen appears to have been again seized with a serious illness, and this also may have tended to delay the maturing of any of the different plans which had been suggested; but, as spring advanced, the chivalrous liberators resumed their exertions.

One of George Douglas's schemes was to introduce into the Castle a large box, under the pretence that it contained papers and other articles of importance which the Queen required. The intention being that the Queen, after arranging for the box being safely re-transported to the shore, should secret herself within it before it was sent off. This scheme does not seem to have been a very practicable one, and apparently it had gone no further than mere preliminary discussion between George Douglas and his sharp-witted assistant Willie Douglas, who at once pointed out the impracticability of the proposed plan, and suggested instead the simpler, although bolder device of getting the Queen out of the Castle openly, and under the eyes of everyone, in the disguise of the washerwoman who regularly went to and fro between Kinross and the Castle.

Willie Douglas's suggestion was adopted, and notice was duly given to the Queen's supporters to hold themselves in readiness for the day fixed for the enterprise. Lady Douglas, unable to have the additional washing required for the captive and her attendants performed on the Castle Island, was in the habit of giving out the linen to a laundress residing in Kinross, who came to the Castle on stated days for the purpose of receiving the soiled linen. The contemplated scheme was duly communicated to the Queen, and the time chosen for the enterprise was the 25th March, being the day for the customary visit of the laundress to Her Majesty's chamber. By an arrangement with the laundress she was easily induced to lend her dress for the occasion, and the Queen having put it on drew a muffler over her face, and, carrying the "fardel" of linen in her arms, she passed out of the Castle unsuspected, and walking down to the shore took her seat in the boat. One of the boatmen, however, having in jest attempted to remove the hood which enveloped the head of the supposed washerwoman, the Queen, in trying to prevent this exposed her hands to view, and their delicacy and whiteness at once disclosed to the boatmen the real state of matters, and they positively refused to row her to the opposite shore. This incident is related by Sir William Drury in a letter written by him to Cecil on the 3rd of April, nine days after the event, and he mentions that the royal prisoner, had she made good her escape, knew where to find her friends, for that George Douglas, John Sempil, and John Beton were in waiting for her.

At this time, and probably in consequence of his participation in this well planned and all but successful effort, Willie Douglas unfortunately found himself ignominiously expelled from the Castle. Various circumstances appear to have aroused Sir William Douglas's suspicion, for, mingled with the shrewdness and natural cleverness by which Willie was characterised, there appears to have been a very decided dash of recklessness. The first element of suspicion arose from the frequency with which Willie, in the course of gambling transactions, to which the youth was strongly addicted, exhibited pieces of gold which the Queen in her free-handed liberality had bestowed upon him, and in addition to this, he had allowed himself to be seen by the Laird's daughter and niece, not only talking secretly with the Queen but even delivering letters to her. These circumstances being duly reported to Sir William, he subjected Willie Douglas to a searching examination, in the course of which the latter was compelled to admit that he had been induced by George to aid him in his attempts to set the Queen at liberty, although he feigned entire ignorance as to the details of the contemplated scheme. In turning Willie Douglas away from the Castle Sir William considered it necessary to send a letter to his brother George, again warning him in the plainest terms as he valued his life, never to come near the Castle or the village of Kinross.

The expulsion of Willie Douglas from the Castle was a very serious check in the further prosecution of the scheme for the Queen's liberation, and must have well nigh caused the captive herself to renounce all hopes of ever effecting her escape, more especially when she found that the person appointed as Willie's successor, to take charge of the boats, was a member of the garrison who had already made himself obnoxious to her by the officious zeal with which he had constituted himself a spy on her every action.

In a touching appeal addressed by her to her mother-in-law the Queen of France, and dated "from my Prison the last day of March," we find the following expression of hopelessness and despair :—"I am in so miserable a state that I am unable to offer my service to you, and as for my good will, that is at all times devoted to you. I have with great difficulty de- spatched the bearer to inform you of my misery, and to supplicate you to have pity upon me." On the same day and by the same bearer (John Beton) the following letter was forwarded to the Archbishop of Glasgow :—

"MONSIEUR DE GLASGOW—Your brother will tell you of my miserable condition, and I beseech you to present him and his letters, interceding as far as you can in my favour. He will tell you more, for I have neither paper nor time to write further, only to pray the King, the Queen, and my Uncle, to burn my letters, for if it was known that I had written it will cost the life of many, and put my own in jeopardy and make me be guarded more strictly. God have you in his care and give me patience.

"From my Prison this last of March,

"Your old very good mistress and friend,

"MARIE R. (now prisoner)."

Indeed but for the services of her faithful attendant, Maria Courcelles, who seems to have been the means by which these letters were conveyed to Beton, the Queen, at this crisis, must have regarded herself as utterly cut off from all communication with her adherents, and the bitterness of this feeling would be much increased by the knowledge she possessed of the success which had already attended George Douglas's efforts to secure the hearty co-operation of the nobles who still espoused her cause. Fortunately the recent attempt at escape does not appear to have affected her treatment personally by Sir William Douglas or his mother, or to have curtailed the restricted liberty she had hitherto enjoyed within the limits of the Castle island. On the contrary Sir William, with a consideration for his illustrious prisoner which one would scarcely have expected from him, and which clearly indicates that he was of a remarkable easy and unsuspicious disposition, even relieved the tedium of her confinement by taking her with him on occasional boating excursions on the lake; and it shows how keenly George Douglas was on the alert, in watching the Queen's movements, and in taking advantage of every opportunity that was afforded him, when we find that a plan was actually formed for securing her liberation on one of these occasions. It was suggested that the Queen should induce Sir William to land on St Serf's Island for the purpose of hawking, and that George Douglas and his followers, who were to secrete themselves in the ruins of St Serf's Monastery for the purpose, should at a favourable moment rush out, and having overpowered Sir William and his boatmen, carry off the Queen to a place of safety. This project does not appear to have been definitely adopted, but the fact of its being entertained shows how intently every movement in the Castle was watched, and how prominent a place the Queen's liberation now occupied in the minds of her supporters. Nor were they singular in thus regarding the projected escape as the all-important topic, for it occupied to an equally engrossing extent the thoughts even of Sir William Douglas and his household and retainers. It formed a frequent subject of discussion not only among the servants and members of the garrison, but even between the Queen and old Lady Douglas, who repeatedly and earnestly urged the Queen to abandon her attempt, on the grounds that if successful, it would only lead to the ruin of the whole Douglas family, whereas in time some good understanding would certainly be brought about between Her Majesty and Lord Moray, by which Her Majesty's wishes would be fully attained without the slightest risk or injury to any one. With remarkable tact and cleverness the Queen discussed her contemplated liberation with the utmost frankness, and plainly stated that so long as she was detained there against her will and unjustly, she would do her best by every means in her power to escape, but the very candour and freedom with which she discussed the matter threw Lady Douglas and her family entirely off their guard, and led them to believe that no definite plan of escape could really be in contemplation, otherwise she would not have disclosed her determination so openly.

So much indeed were the minds of the garrison occupied by ideas of the escape that, on one occasion when Sir William Douglas and his prisoner landed at the Castle after one of their boating excursions, they found the servants actually amusing themselves with a pretended assault on the Castle for the purpose of liberating the Queen—the Lady of Lochleven herself being one of the interested spectators of the sport. Some of the party in a boat formed the attacking force, while the remainder from the shore defended the Castle, and endeavoured to prevent the others from effecting a landing by pelting them with pieces of turf or other similarly " mild " and innocuous missiles. These the besiegers caught and threw back again among their opponents; but apparently this mode of retaliation was much too tame to suit the bellicose tastes of Will Drysdale, the chief officer of the garrison, to whom special reference has already been made, and he, in order to impart a more real aspect to the pretended attack, took up a long harquebus lying in the boat, which he fancied was only loaded with powder, and fired it point blank among the people on the shore. Unfortunately the gun was loaded with pellets and two of the men of the garrison were seriously wounded in the thigh and had to be placed under the professional care of the Queen's private surgeon, who, finding that his patients were two of the most persistent and vigilant spies on the Queen's movements—one of them being the man who as Willie Douglas's successor had been intrusted with the control of the boats—took the precaution to confine them both strictly to their beds as long as he possibly could.

So soon as George Douglas heard of this accident he at once resolved to avail himself of the favourable opportunity it afforded for carrying out his long contemplated project, and as he had hitherto refrained from replying to the letter he had received from his brother, at the time of Willie Douglas's expulsion, he now made that letter an excuse for resuming friendly communication with the members of the Lochleven household. He accordingly came openly to Kinross, and annouced to his mother and brother that he had resolved to leave his native country and seek his fortunes in France, and he stated that he had come for the double purpose of bidding them farewell, and of obtaining from the Queen letters of recommendation to her powerful friends and relatives in that country. This explanation was an ingenious one, and both Lady Douglas and Sir William accepted of it with the most implicit faith. His pretended resolution caused both of them much distress, for they were warmly attached to him, and were strongly opposed to his leaving his native country. They tried their utmost to induce him to abandon his intention, and urged him rather to take up his abode with his half-brother Moray, and attach himself to his rising fortunes; but this he positively refused to do. In her maternal distress Lady Douglas even appealed to the Queen to aid her by persuading her son to yield to her wishes, and at her solicitation the Queen wrote to him on the subject, apparently in the spirit his mother wished, but in reality urging him in covert terms to hasten on his arrangements for her escape.

George Douglas does not appear to have been allowed at this time to come to the Castle, but while resident at Kinross he had free and uninterrupted intercourse with his mother and sisters, and he seems to have turned to good account the opportunities thus afforded him of bringing his plans to maturity. Deprived of Willie Douglas's aid, there was no one within the Castle walls who could co-operate with him, and this formed a serious disadvantage, for the great obstacle to the carrying out of their scheme was the difficulty in finding a means of egress from the courtyard of the Castle at the only time of the day at which escape was at all practicable.

There was then, as there is now, only one gate to the courtyard, and as George Douglas well knew from his familiarity with the daily domestic routine of the establishment, the key of this gate formed, both literally and figuratively, "the key to the position," and he also knew the jealousy and care with which Sir William Douglas kept this key during the only period of the day when it could by any possibility be made available for facilitating the escape. During the day the gate no doubt stood unlocked and open, but this was of no advantage to their scheme, as the Queen was never allowed to go beyond the courtyard unless accompanied by one or more of the members of the household. During the night too, the facility was still further diminished, as it was the custom to lock the gate regularly at seven o'clock in the evening, when Sir William and his household sat down to supper, and on Sir William taking his seat at the supper table the key was deposited on the table at his side, and remained in his possession until next morning, when the hour for re-opening the gate arrived.   No one knew these details better than George Douglas did, and it was therefore clear that the Queen's escape could only be successfully carried into effect during the supper hour, when the warders were for at least half-an-hour relieved from duty, and also that some means of egress from the court-yard other than the gate must if possible be found.

The only other possible exit from the courtyard was by the projecting window in the outer wall of the south-east tower On examining this window, the sides of which are now much broken and destroyed, there is no appearance of its ever having been fitted with iron stanchions, and, trusting to its height from the ground, and still more to the door of the tower affording a means by which it could, when necessary, be completely and securely shut off from all communication with the courtyard, it probably never had any such protection from without.   It is not likely that the door of this tower was secured at the hour when the gate was locked, and there was therefore nothing to prevent any one in the courtyard from gaining easy access to the tower, from which the window above referred to afforded an inconvenient, but still not an extremely difficult means of exit.   At all events it is clear that George Douglas, in his inability to devise other means for enabling the Queen to find her way beyond the ramparts of the Castle, indicated this window as her only means of escape, and, as the sill of the window is fully eight feet from the ground, there was involved in the scheme a risk which occasioned some little hesitation.

In leaping from such a height, it was feared that the Queen might possibly sustain an injury, which, although in itself trifling, might disable her from proceeding further in her flight, and, in order to remove all doubt on this point, it was suggested that she should put the practicability of the scheme to a practical preliminary test. Accordingly she and her attendants, while amusing themselves in the garden, resolved that in order to try the experiment without arousing suspicion, one of the attendants, while pursued by the Queen, should leap a wall in the garden (probably the still existing wall or terrace enclosing the garden) nearly similar in height to that of the sill of the window, and that the Queen should follow her example. The attendant in leaping from the top of the wall stumbled and would have fallen had she not been caught by one of the gentlemen of the household, and the Queen, deterred by her mishap, did not attempt the leap: The attendant was found to have sustained serious injury in one of the joints of her foot, and afraid that a similar accident might befall her, and prevent her from leaving the island, the Queen felt herself compelled to point out this risk to George Douglas, and she arranged that if any thing of this kind occurred, notice would be given to him by a light displayed from the window of her apartment in order that he and his confederates might at once make good their escape.

Driven to extremities by this communication George Douglas seems to have realised that, unless by some means possession of the key of the courtyard gate could be secured, all their labour was likely to prove in vain, and he accordingly resolved to make a vigorous effort to get Willie Douglas reinstated in his former position in the Castle. Through one of his sisters he succeeded in inducing Sir William Douglas once more to take Willie into favour, and there was the less difficulty in effecting this result owing to the man who had been discharging Willie's

duties being still disabled by his gunshot wound, and owing
probably to Sir William himself having sadly missed many of
the personal services which his young protégé had been in the
habit of rendering.

Willie Douglas returned to the Castle on the 30th April,
and the Queen must once more have begun to hope that the efforts
of her liberators were to be crowned with success.   Schooled,
however, by former failures, she does not appear to have permitted herself to indulge in too sanguine anticipations, for, on
the day after Willie's return, she writes to her mother-in-law, the
Queen of France, in the following terms :—

"LOCHLEVEN, 1st May 1568.

"MADAME,—I send to you the bearer on this occasion of my writing
to the King your son, that he may tell you more at length, for I am so
closely guarded that I have no leisure but when they are at dinner, or
sleeping, when I rise stealthily, for their girls lie with me.   This bearer will
tell you all.   I entreat you to give him credit, and to reward him and
those he will present to you, according as you love me.   I implore you
both to have pity on me, for if you take me not hence by force I shall
never come out, I am certain.   But if you would send troops, all Scotland
would revolt from Moray and Morton on perceiving you took the matter
heartily.   I beseech you to give credit to the bearer, and to hold me in
your good favour.   I pray God that He give you His and the happiness
I desire for you."

"From my Prison this 1st May,

"Your very humble and very obedient Daughter,
"MARIE."

"A la Reine de France, Madame ma belle mere."

The following letter, also writen by her on the same day to
Queen Elizabeth, is important and instructive, for it seems to
indicate that even at this early stage she anticipated the fatal

necessity which ultimately induced her to throw herself on the protection of her treacherous kinswoman :—

"From Lochleven this 1st of May.

"MADAME, MY GOOD SISTER.—The length of my weary imprisonment, and the wrongs I have received from those on whom I have conferred so many benefits, are less annoying to me than not having it in my power to acquaint you with the reality of my calamities, and the injuries that have been done to me in various ways. Therefore, having found means to send a line to you by a faithful servant, to whom I have confided my whole mind, I entreat you to give the same credit to him as to myself. It may please you to remember that you have told me several times, 'that, on receiving that ring you gave me, you would assist me in any time of trouble.' You know that Moray has seized all I have, and those who had the keeping of some of those things have been ordered not to deliver any of them to me. Robert Melville, at any rate, to whom I have often secretly sent for this ring, as my most precious jewel, says 'he dare not let me have it.' Therefore I implore you, on receiving this letter, to have compassion on your good sister and cousin, and believe that you have not a more affectionate relative in the world. You should also consider the importance of the example practised against me, not only to sovereigns but to those of lower degree.

"I entreat you to be careful that no one knows that I have written to you, for it would cause me to be treated worse than I am now, and they boast of being informed by their friends of all that you say and do.

"Believe the bearer of this as you would myself. God keep you from misfortunes, and grant me patience and His grace that I may one day recount my calamities to yourself, when I will tell you more than I dare to write, which may prove of no small service to yourself.

"Your obliged and affectionate good Sister and Cousin,

"MARY R."

"From my Prison, this first of May."

The first of these letters was probably written early in the morning of the 1st of May, before she had been informed that her projected liberation had been definitely fixed for the next day; but the second letter, addressed to Queen Elizabeth, appears to have been written not only in the knowledge that a crisis in her fate was impending, but even under a realisation, more or less distinct, of what might possibly form the sequel to her escape. It is impossible otherwise to account for her extreme anxiety at this special moment to recover the talisman which was expected to have the wonderful effect of opening even Queen Elizabeth's hard and obdurate heart to her. That the ring was afterwards recovered we know, for after the disaster at Langside we find that Lord Herries was sent on in advance into England as the bearer of a diamond ring and a frantic appeal for Queen Elizabeth's protection—an appeal which alas proved to be as futile as it was frantic.

The same day Lady Margaret Douglas had gone to Kinross for the purpose of having a parting interview with her son George, previous to his supposed departure for France; and, on returning to the Castle, she, by her son's instructions, redelivered to the Queen the pearl ear-ring sometime previously given by her to him, explaining that one of the boatmen had found the ear-ring and had offered to sell it to her son George, but as he recognized it as an ornament the Queen was in the habit of wearing, he had taken possession of it and had kept it until he had an opportunity of restoring it to her. Well did the Queen know the secret intelligence which the jewel was intended to convey, and it must have cost her no slight effort to receive it at Lady Douglas's hands with that calmness and composure which the circumstances required. Racked by feelings of alternate hope and despondency the royal captive that night laid her head on her pillow for the last time within a Scotch prison, and passed a long sleepless night of feverish anxiety.

The arrangements of her friends were in every way practical and complete. George Douglas was already on the spot, and was residing in the Inn at Kinross. Beton had a day or two previously gone to Seton to arrange details with Lord Seton, and notice had already been sent to all the Queen's principal supporters to hold themselves in readiness at a moment's notice. Seton and Beton, accompanied by a band of fifty carefully selected cavaliers, were to cross the Forth next morning, and to lurk in the neighbourhood of Lochleven until the hour of escape arrived, in order to be ready to form a body-guard for the Queen the moment she landed on the shore at Kinross. In the course of her exciting life Queen Mary was doomed to pass through many a painful experience, but the last night she spent in Kinross-shire, with its fluctuating hopes and doubts, was probably not the least trying ordeal in her career.

CHAPTER VI.

QUEEN MARY'S ESCAPE.

"Hope like the gleaming taper's light,
   Adorns and cheers the way."
                              GOLDSMITH.

"And yet the path our hopes illume,
   May prove the pathway to our doom."
                              ANON.

ON Sunday the 2nd of May 1568 Queen Mary must have risen from her sleepless couch with a depressing sense of the long weary hours of restless anxiety which lay before her, and at the same time with bright anticipations of all that the future had in store for her. Fully sensible of the delicate and difficult part she had to play, she was also sensible of the vigilant eyes which from morning to night surrounded her, and of the jealousy with which her every movement was watched. Within the Castle walls there was no lack of spies, consisting not merely of Sir William Douglas and his retainers, whose duty it was to keep sure watch and ward over their captive, but even of the very ladies of the household, who permitted themselves also to be impressed into that ungracious service. These latter were both numerous and zealous enough to call into requisition the Queen's acuteness and tact, and her marvellous readiness of resource. They consisted not only of the Dowager Lady Douglas and her daughter-in-law, Sir William's wife—whose special duty it seems

to have been to constitute herself as the inseparable companion
of the captive—but also of Sir William's daughter and niece,
who have already been referred to as regularly sharing the same
sleeping apartment with the Queen, and ready at all times to
mount guard when the services of Lady Douglas or Sir William's
wife were not available. These are the only members of the
Douglas family specially referred to by Nau as then resident
within the Castle, but in addition to them there may have been
included in the household, one or more of Sir William Douglas's
sisters. These were not fewer than seven in number, and on
account of their stature and elegance, they were generally styled
the "seven fair porches of Lochleven;" and of them six were
still unmarried, the seventh being married to Lord Lindsay, which
probably accounts for his having been conjoined with his brother-
in-law Sir William Douglas as one of the custodians of the
Queen. Miss Strickland, in her interesting but extremely one-
sided "Life of Queen Mary," assumes that the Countess of Buchan,
who was married to Sir William's younger brother, also formed
one of the regular inmates of the Castle, but the only apparent
grounds for this assumption is the fact that the Countess, sometime previous to the Queen's imprisonment, gave birth there to
her first child, an event which does not necessarily imply that it
formed her permanent abode. The probability rather is that Sir
William's maiden sisters, and the Countess of Buchan, with her
husband Robert Douglas, occupied "The New House of Lochleven," along with Lady Margaret Douglas their mother, while Sir
William and his wife and children and niece resided within the
Castle; nor is this probability at all inconsistent with the fact
that Lady Margaret Douglas so frequently appears on the scene,
for the distance between "The New House of Lochleven," and
the Castle Island being less than a mile, it could easily be

traversed by a boat, in moderate weather, in ten minutes or quarter of an hour. This probability too is strengthened by the fact that the accommodation within the Castle, if the present ruins indicate, as we may reasonably assume that they do, the whole buildings that then existed on the Island, is utterly inadequate for so large a household, in addition to the Queen and her attendants, and the garrison required for the protection of the stronghold.

The Queen had flattered herself that the spies on her movements at this critical period had been materially diminished, owing to Sir William Douglas's wife having recently given birth to a child; and the escape had been specially planned to take place before she was again astir, but her recovery had been more rapid than was anticipated, and to the serious increase of the poor captive's difficulties Sir William's wife was that day for the first time able to resume her ungracious and undignified duty as assistant turnkey. Another still more vexatious disappointment that day awaited the Queen in the untimeous return to the Castle of the chief officer of the garrison— Will Drysdale, a worthy to whom special reference has more than once been already made, and whose absence at this time she imagined she had satisfactorily provided for. Drysdale seems to have been an inveterate enemy to the Queen, and it afforded him a malicious pleasure to act the part of spy on her movements, and to thwart every scheme which she had hitherto devised. In order to relieve herself from his watchful eye, she had resorted to the ingenious device of presenting him, in a simulated fit of generosity, with a gift of money in the shape of a draft on the State Treasurer, of which Drysdale could only receive payment by going personally to Edinburgh; and, in order to make assurance doubly sure, she had commissioned him to bring to her at the sametime from Holyrood some articles of which she pretended to be in urgent and immediate want. In the private written order for these articles, addressed to an official on whose fidelity she knew she could depend, she had introduced a special injunction that Drysdale was to be detained in Edinburgh as long as possible, and although this injunction had been faithfully given effect to, still it had not been found possible to prevent Drysdale from returning on the very day on which his absence was most essential.

So circumstanced and surrounded, the Queen's first and engrossing aim was to devise means for concentrating the attention of Sir William Douglas and his numerous and watchful household on something as widely as possible apart from her and her aspirations for freedom ; and with this view she had arranged with Willie Douglas that he, under the pretence probably of celebrating his return to the Castle, should invite the whole household to a déjeûner, for which she secretly provided him with the requisite means. This entertainment was purposely fixed to take place in a part of the Castle farthest removed from the courtyard gate, and no doubt this particular spot had been selected for the simple reason that it confined the guests to the portion of the building from which it was impossible for them to see the shore at Kinross, or to have their attention drawn to any unwonted or suspicious movements that might, during the earlier period of the day, take place in that direction. It is not to be supposed that the Queen had more than a mere vague and general idea of the mode in which her chivalrous liberators were to find their way to the scene of the contemplated escape, and she knew well that the mere sight of a few horsemen in the neighbourhood of the loch would at once create an amount of insatiable curiosity and conjecture, which might ultimately lead to the discovery of the whole plot.

It cannot be doubted that, in their insular habitation, the pleasure of watching all that transpired on the surrounding shores of the lake must, to the inmates of the Castle, have formed a never failing resource, as it afforded them something new to interest and engage their thoughts, and no doubt this craving for any excitement, however mild, which tended to beguile the tedium of their life, accounts for the readiness with which Sir William gave his good-natured consent to Willie's festivity, and the popular reception which it met with among the household generally.

Both the Queen and Sir William Douglas attended the entertainment, and, during a part of the proceedings Willie Douglas, as "The Abbot of Unreason" in a pastime which Sir Walter Scott refers to in "The Abbot" as forming one of the popular amusements of the period, presented the Queen and each of his other guests with a branch, and specially pledged the Queen to follow him wherever he went during the remainder of the day. It is difficult to see what bearing this pledge, playfully extorted from the Queen in presence of the whole guests, had upon her contemplated escape, but probably it was intended by her acute and ingenious liberator to serve as a plausible explanation and excuse, in the event of his being afterwards intercepted in the very act of conducting the Queen out of the Castle. In that emergency he may possibly have contemplated resorting to the plea, that they were merely carrying out the frolic begun in the earlier part of the day, and that the Queen was only fulfilling the pledge which she had then given him in sport. The Queen remained as long as possible among the rest of the guests, for she knew that her presence there would detain both Sir William Douglas and his wife at her side, and past experience had possibly taught her

Plate VI

LOCHLEVEN CASTLE.

that they were never less suspicious than when she was actually in their presence, and bringing to bear upon them the tact and ready wit which never seemed to fail her in conversation. Willie, as host and master of ceremonies, seems to have exerted himself to the utmost for the amusement of his guests, and so well did he succeed that "everyone laughed at him as if he were drunk or a very simpleton" *(comme d'un homme enyvré ou fort simple.)*

Having prolonged the "revel" as long as she possibly could, the Queen retired to her own apartment under the pretence that she required rest, and she threw herself upon her bed while Sir William's wife, who had accompanied her to her apartment, sat near, engaged in gossiping with the woman who kept the inn at Kinross, whose presence at the Castle on that particular day was no doubt connected in some way with the entertainment in the earlier portion of the day. Among other items of local intelligence communicated by this woman, the Queen overheard her mentioning that several horsemen had that day passed through Kinross with Lord Seton among them, and that they said they were on their way to an assize court, and also that George Douglas was still staying in Kinross. To these items of intelligence the Queen must have listened with greedy ears, and no doubt they created in her mind an irresistible desire to get out of doors in order to see for herself if any unwonted stir was yet visible on the western shore.

She therefore, about five o'clock in the afternoon, after she had taken off her ordinary dress, and put on a kirtle belonging to one of her attendants, and enveloped herself in a long mantle so as to conceal the alteration in her apparel, went into the garden, from which she could see the people walking on the shore at Kinross. Here she was joined by old Lady Douglas, with whom she for some time walked and conversed;

and while so engaged, Lady Douglas saw a body of men on
horseback riding along the road on the western shore leading
towards Kinross, and this excited so powerfully her suspicions,
that she raised an out-cry, and expressed her determination
to send a messenger at once to ascertain who they were.
Surmising that the horsemen formed a detachment of her
liberators, the Queen at once saw the necessity for diverting the
old lady's attention, and with this view she ingeniously entered
into a long recapitulation of her grounds of complaint against
Lady Douglas's favourite son, the Earl of Moray, for his base
and unnatural treatment of her ; and on this topic she continued
to engross Lady Douglas's attention until the hour for supper
arrived.   In fact, in order to afford time for the due completion
of all the arrangements for her escape, she contrived to delay
supper till after the usual hour—seven o'clock—and it was
only when Sir William Douglas himself came to conduct her to
her apartments that she returned within the walls of the Castle.

On conducting the Queen to her sitting-room a circumstance
attracted Sir William's attention which, but for her inimitable
tact, might have led to an instant exposure of the contemplated
scheme.   As Sir William stood gazing out of the window on
the east side of the Queen's apartment (the window over the
entrance doorway of the tower) he noticed Willie Douglas at
the landing place almost immediately below the window, engaged
in some mysterious manipulation of the chains of the boats.
Willie was in fact at that moment endeavouring to provide
against all risk of immediate pursuit, by inserting little pegs
of wood into the chains by which the boats, with the exception
of the one he intended to use, were attached to the pier, in order
to prevent these from being easily unfastened.   On perceiving
Willie thus engaged Sir William was angry and challenged

him roughly from the window, calling him a fool; and the Queen, fearful as to what might result if Sir William discovered the real nature and object of Willie's industry, at once pretended that she felt very unwell, and entreated Sir William to bring her some wine. As there was no one in the apartment but Sir William and herself he went at once to bring the wine, and in doing so quite forgot what he had seen and took no further notice of the matter.

According to his invariable habit, Sir William himself waited upon the Queen while she was at supper, and it was only after she had finished her repast that he betook himself to the room immediately below her apartments for the purpose of supping there with his wife and the whole of his household. The Queen's inveterate enemy, Will Drysdale, was also in the room during supper, but he retired immediately after his master, leaving the Queen and her two attendants, along with Sir William's daughter and niece, as the sole occupants of the apartment. In order to elude the vigilant *espionage* of these girls, the Queen, immediately after finishing supper, went into a room above her own which was occupied by her surgeon. She pretended that her reason for going there was to pray, and, with that deep devotional feeling which formed so prominent a feature in her extraordinary character, she did engage in fervent prayer on the verge of this crisis in her fate. While in this room, she disguised herself still further by putting on a hood such as was then worn by the country women of the district, and she caused one of her attendants who was to accompany her in her flight (probably Jane Kennedy) to dress herself in a similar disguise. The other attendant (Maria Courcelles) had been left in the room below with the two young girls, in order to engage their attention and prevent them from following the Queen.

Meantime the Laird had seated himself at supper, and that evening he fortunately, for some unexplained reason, caused to be closed the window in the west wall of the dining hall, which he invariably kept open in order that, when seated at table, he might see any boat approaching the Castle from the direction of Kinross, and he thus unwittingly aided in the success of the escape. Willie Douglas, immediately before the hour arrived for locking the Castle gate, had, with prudent forethought, and in anticipation of his possible failure to secure possession of the key of the courtyard gate, provided for the Queen an alternative mode of escape by placing two oars side by side with their ends resting on the sill of the window of the round tower, so as to assist her in her descent from the window, should she be compelled to adopt that means of egress; and having completed this arrangement and otherwise satisfied himself that everything else was in readiness, he hastened to render his usual service to Sir William at the supper table. While engaged in discharging this duty, and in the act of handing the wine to Sir William, he found a favourable opportunity for gaining possession of the key of the outer gate. This extremely delicate manœuvre he managed very adroitly by dropping, as if accidentally, a napkin over the key as it lay on the table at Sir William's side, and in lifting the napkin he lifted the key also. There was probably seated at the supper table one person—the Queen's medical attendant—who, fully cognisant of all the plans for the contemplated escape, must have watched with intense interest Willie's dexterous movements, and it can easily be imagined with what eagerness he would bring into play any conversational gifts he possessed, in order to divert the attention of Sir William and his household from the little drama that was being acted under their very eyes.

Page 10.

Lochleven Castle.

North Elevation

West Elevation

South Elevation

East Elevation

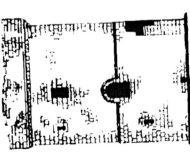

ELEVATIONS & SECTION OF SQUARE KEEP.

Plate VII.

The moment he was possessed of the key Willie left the room, and on emerging from the doorway of the tower on his way to unlock the gate, he signalled to the Queen's attendant who was on the watch at one of the upper windows, that the all important moment had arrived. On receiving this intelligence the Queen, accompanied by her attendant, instantly descended the spiral stair in the south-east corner of the tower until she reached the corridor adjoining the dining hall, and then gliding swiftly and silently along this corridor past the very door of the apartment in which her custodian was seated at supper, she reached the entrance doorway of the tower and passed down the long flight of stone steps which led from this doorway to the level of the courtyard. The foundations of this outside stair are still distinctly visible, and they show clearly that the lower portion of the stair projected considerably into the courtyard in order to make the ascent less abrupt, and it was probably at the point where the steps protruded beyond the line of the south wall of the tower that the Queen found, to her dismay, that she and her companion were walking directly into view of several of the servants of the household who were passing and repassing in the courtyard. Shrinking back once more behind the corner of the tower, she stood near the entrance doorway, uncertain whether to proceed or retreat, but an instant's reflection convinced her that there was no alternative, and rapidly continuing her descent, she crossed a portion of the yard in sight of the whole of them and passed out at the courtyard gate, which Willie Douglas had by this time unlocked, and at which he stood impatiently awaiting her. No sooner were she and her attendant outside the gate than Willie quietly relocked it, and throwing the key into the mouth of a cannon that stood near, he ran swiftly down to the pier on the east side of the Island to unfasten and prepare the boat. While he was so engaged, the Queen and her companion stood for a few long and anxious moments close under the shelter of the rampart, in order to prevent themselves from being observed from any of the Castle windows, and immediately on receiving from their liberator the signal that all was ready, they quickly followed his example, and got on board the boat.

At first the Queen, in accordance with the injunctions which had been specially impressed upon her, crouched down in the bottom of the boat, partly to avoid being seen, and partly to avoid any risk of injury in the event of their being fired at from the Castle walls. It would appear that the escape was witnessed and connived at by some of the inferior domestics within the Castle, for some "washerwomen" who were engaged on the shore of the Island saw the Queen stepping into the boat, and one of them even showed by signs that she recognised her, but Willie Douglas, calling to the woman by name, told her to hold her tongue. So soon as they had rounded the north extremity of the Island, and had attained a safe distance from the Castle, the Queen arose from the bottom of the boat, and, as a signal to her friends on the shore at Kinross, she waved aloft her white veil bordered with red. This was the preconcerted signal by which she was to announce her escape, and it had for sometime been eagerly and intently watched for by many a longing eye.

Lord Seton and his followers had, since four o'clock in the afternoon lain in concealment within a secluded hollow on Benarty Hill, from which they could, without risk of being themselves seen, overlook whatever transpired on the lake This spot had been selected for the purpose by Beton after a careful survey of the locality, and Lord Seton and his party were guided to it by James Wardlaw, who was probably some well known local partisan, as Kirkaldy of Grange, in writing to Sir William Douglas on 1st June 1568 with information as to the parties implicated in the escape, seems to imagine that he sufficiently indicated Wardlaw's identity by simply mentioning his name. Beton himself, accompanied by ten of his men, after parting with Seton and his companions, continued his journey northwards to Kinross, which he reached about five o'clock, and it was no doubt this mounted band which Lady Douglas had seen entering that town, while she was walking with the Queen in the Castle garden.

On arriving at the Inn at Kinross, Beton had found George Douglas in waiting, and, in order to allay any suspicion that might be entertained by the people at the Inn, he, on his arrival, openly announced to the landlord that he was on his way to Glasgow, and as George Douglas stated that he also was about to go there to join his brother the Regent, it was arranged that they would become travelling companions on the day following. While he and Douglas were supping together in the Inn, Beton stated that he was suffering from headache, and suggested that they should go out for an airing along the shore of the loch. Scarcely had they gone a few yards when they, probably from the rising ground which now forms the southern boundary of the policy of Kinross House, came in full view of the loch ; and, after an interval of anxious and painful expectancy they at length had the intense satisfaction of seeing the boat gliding rapidly out from the Castle Island, and immediately afterwards they observed the Queen's signal. At once Beton ordered his men to mount, and, hurrying down to the " New House of Lochleven " along with George Douglas, they saddled two of the best horses in the Laird's stable, standing close to the shore, and led them down to a pier which for the purpose of convenient communication with the Castle, was constructed within a few yards from the house. This pier must have been nearly opposite to the present "Fish Gate" at Kinross House, and about mid-distance between the "New House" and the Kirk of Kinross. That a pier existed at this spot in olden times is a fact well established, not only by local tradition and belief, but even by the actual necessity arising from the relative position of the Castle on the one hand, and of "the New House of Lochleven" on the other; and it must equally be regarded as a point beyond question that Willie Douglas and the other liberators of the Queen would select as her landing place the very nearest available spot at which she could disembark with ease and comfort—a desideratum only attainable on Lochleven, owing to the extreme and unvarying flatness of its margin, by the construction of an artificial landing place, extending for several yards into the shallow water.

When the boat was still a little way from the pier, Willie Douglas, to his dismay, discovered that a man fully armed was waiting to receive them, and not recognising him, he, apprehensive of danger, stopped the boat at a safe distance from the shore. The man, however, spoke to him, and Willie, having from his voice recognised him as one of George Douglas's followers, unhesitatingly rowed the boat ashore. By this time George Douglas and Beton had also reached the pier, and they were the first to receive the Queen on her stepping out of the boat. Beton's men having now also arrived, the whole party, so soon as the Queen was mounted, prepared to ride off as quickly as possible, but this the Queen positively refused to allow, until she saw her youthful liberator, Willie Douglas, also safely seated on horseback. Probably he was provided with the horse intended for the Queen's female attendant, for she alone was left behind, but she was directed to follow them as soon as she could find an outfit. This arrangement having been duly completed, the party at once rode off towards Queensferry, about fifteen miles to the south of Kinross—where Beton had already provided means for their being ferried across the Forth—and they had scarce accomplished the first mile of their journey ere they were joined by Lord Seton and his companions, who had ridden rapidly from their place of concealment on Benarty Hill so soon as they perceived the Queen's signal.

Nau relates that the Queen's escape was viewed with satisfaction by the inhabitants of Kinross, and that they blessed her and prayed for her safety as she rode through amongst them, no one attempting to stop her progress, not even the uncle of the Laird of Lochleven, who, among others recognised her, and seemed pleased to witness her liberation from her long captivity; and the fact that the escape was witnessed by so many of the inhabitants of Kinross, is a further proof that the spot indicated as the place where she landed was really the scene of that interesting historical event. She and her companions, in finding their way from the landing place to the public road to Queensferry, must necessarily have passed along the present " Kirkgate," and round the west side of the loch by Sandport, and they would thus ride through group after group of the villagers enjoying then, as their successors do still, their usual Sunday evening stroll along that favourite resort. One can easily imagine how readily and spontaneously expressions of kindly sympathy would be elicited from these groups as the mounted cavalcade rode past them, led by Queen Mary herself in all her striking grace and beauty, and flushed with the excitement of long lost liberty regained, and dormant hope re-awakened.

CONCLUSION.

It need not here be told that the gleam of hope which radiated around the unfortunate Queen, as she found herself once more standing in safety and freedom on the shore of Kinross, was as short-lived as it was brilliant. Every schoolboy knows that she regained her liberty only to encounter calamities and disasters still more severe than those which she fondly imagined she was now leaving behind her. Scarcely had a week elapsed ere she found herself stationed on the rising ground at Langside, helplessly witnessing the utter collapse of her last supreme effort, in the total rout of her forces by the better disciplined army of her brother, the Regent Moray. Impelled by the frantic energy of blind desperation, she rode straight from the disastrous field of battle to the English border—a distance of sixty miles—without a halt, and with that fatal and impulsive trustfulness which so often led her astray, she threw herself on the protection of her treacherous kinswoman and bitterest enemy, Queen Elizabeth, by whom she was subjected to fresh indignities and privations, and to a rigorous captivity of nearly twenty years' duration, which was only terminated by the headsman's axe on the scaffold at Fotheringay. Never was unjust doom more nobly met; and by her calm unshrinking fortitude and dignified bearing in her last trying hours, she shed a halo around her name, and proved herself to be both a true heroine and a genuine Queen.

Alike on the field of battle, and during her flight into England, Queen Mary was faithfully attended by a select few of her adherents and personal attendants, who as a special bodyguard devoted themselves to her protection ; and prominent among these are the names of her two youthful liberators, George Douglas and Willie Douglas. Both of them continued for sometime to share the captivity of their Royal Mistress in England, and both had life pensions assigned to them by the Queen, as a reward for their devoted services.

George Douglas, at an early period of Queen Mary's captivity in England, was sent by her on a special mission to France—the ostensible purpose, as explained in Queen Mary's letter to Queen Elizabeth soliciting his passport, being "to enable him to pass some time in France to learn the language, and to be rewarded in some measure by the king my good brother and my uncles by their desire," but the real object was undoubtedly to secure on her behalf the active aid of the Court of France. Douglas seems to have spent a considerable time in Paris, but he was not successful in bringing about any very energetic interposition on the part of France in her favour. During his residence in France he formed a tender attachment there, which, but for the extreme uncertainty of his prospects at that time, would in all probability have culminated in marriage. The Queen interested herself warmly and heartily in his matrimonial prospects, and several of her letters at this period relate to practical efforts she was then making to remove as far as she could the pecuniary difficulties which prevented the union. These efforts, owing to the embarrassed state of her own affairs, led to no satisfactory result, and George Douglas

returned to Scotland unmarried in the year 1571. In 1575 he
again went to France, seeing Queen Mary as he passed through,
England; and on his return to Scotland he married a " Lady
Barery," who is stated to have resided "near Lochleven." In
1580 he is again sent to France—this time as Ambassador
on behalf of Queen Mary's youthful son King James—at whose
Court he must by this time have acquired considerable influence,
for in the following year we find the captive Queen urging
him to induce her son openly to espouse her cause. After
this date George Douglas acquired the Lands of Holenhill
in Fife, and Ashieshiels in Tweeddale; and in 1602 he, under
the title of "Sir George Douglas of Holenhill," was formally
appointed as tutor-at-law to his niece Mary Douglas, Countess
of Buchan, the daughter of his immediate elder brother Robert,
who as previously explained, married Christina Countess of
Buchan. George Douglas at his death left one child—a
daughter—who married Lord Dalhousie, and he thus became
the direct ancestor of one of the noblest of our old Scotch
families.

Of Sir William Douglas, "the Laird of Lochleven," little remains to be told. The escape of the Queen from his custody was
a severe and bitter humiliation to him. On the evening of the
escape, he and his wife and their guests remained unsuspectingly
at the supper table until they were suddenly aroused by Will
Drysdale bursting into the room with the startling announcement that the Queen had disappeared. This intelligence had
been first communicated to Drysdale by Sir William's daughter
and niece, who, becoming impatient for the Queen's return to
her own apartment, had contrived to find their way up-stairs to
the surgeon's room. Instead of the Queen being there, they
found the room in disorder, and the cloak which the Queen had

been wearing thrown carelessly aside. From this and other circumstances they seem to have at once surmised what had occurred, and they rushed down to the dining-hall to communicate their suspicions to Sir William. Encountering Drysdale before they entered the dining-hall, they startled him with the tidings of which they were the bearers, and in an instant the Castle became a scene of wild excitement and fury. Drysdale stormed and raged like a maniac, while even Sir William himself had to be forcibly restrained by his servants in order to prevent him from doing himself bodily injury. In the midst of the turmoil there was heard a thundering at the courtyard gate, and on enquiry —for the gate itself could not be opened in consequence of the key being amissing—it was found that some of the villagers of Kinross had rowed back the boat in which the Queen had escaped, and they not only confirmed the fears already entertained, but also conveyed the further intelligence that the Queen and her companions were already many miles on their journey towards Queensferry. Sir William was much reflected upon for his laxity and easiness in the custody of his prisoner, but it does not appear to have affected injuriously his future career. At the battle of Langside he took a prominent part, and in many of the public events of the next few years his name occasionally crops out ; and about twenty years after the Queen's escape, he, on the execution of the Earl of Morton, to whom he was nearly related, and the subsequent death of Morton's nephew, the Earl of Angus, succeeded as heir of entail to the Earldom of Morton, and the estate of Lochleven thus became, for nearly a century, merged in the extensive Morton possessions.

The ultimate fate of "little Willie Douglas" has not been elucidated so clearly as that of his co-liberator George Douglas. He was included in the Queen's retinue at Carlisle, and afterwards at Bolton, but in the end of the year 1568 he mysteriously disappeared. Queen Mary felt considerable anxiety in regard to him, and, under the impression that he had either been assassinated or captured by her enemies in consequence of the important share he had borne in her liberation from Lochleven, she, on the 2nd February 1569, wrote to her Commissioners telling them of Willie being "tint," and urged them to use every possible effort to find out what had become of him. Willie's "good luck" and ingenuity however, seem still to have clung to him, for not only was he traced out and liberated from prison, but he even ultimately found his way to the Court of France, and remained in Paris for a considerable time. On 15th October 1572, the English Ambassador in France writes that "Willie Douglas departeth into Scotland, who had long conference with the King and Queen mother." His after career is involved in mystery. Apparently the love for adventure and intrigue which he imbibed at Lochleven Castle continued strongly to characterise him in after life, for in 1570 he was supposed to be the medium through whom encouragement and pecuniary aid was secretly conveyed to the rebel subjects of the English Queen during the Northern Rebellion. Whatever may have been his ultimate destiny, his name as the youthful liberator of his unfortunate Queen will ever occupy a prominent place in Scottish History, and his fame will survive that of many of our bravest heroes and most distinguished statesmen. As long indeed as the romantic career and the deeply tragic fate of Mary Queen of Scots continues to appeal to the sympathy and interest of humanity at large, so long will be preserved from oblivion the names of the two Kinross-shire youths who so chivalrously devoted not only their future prospects, but even their very lives to her liberation from her long captivity within the walls of Lochleven Castle.

APPENDIX.

I. EXTRACTS FROM MEMORIALS OF THE REIGN OF QUEEN MARY BY CLAUDE NAU, HER SECRETARY. *Translated by the Rev. Joseph Stevenson, S.J., from the original now in the British Museum.*

QUEEN'S JOURNEY FROM HOLYROOD TO LOCHLEVEN.

IN the middle of the supper the Earl of Morton, who all the time had been standing behind the Queen's chair, asked an esquire of the stable whether the horses were ready. He ordered the dishes to be removed from the table, and told the Queen to prepare to mount on horseback. . . . . Two *femmes-de-chambre* only were appointed to attend to her, all the rest crying and entreating that they might follow their mistress. . . . .

The Queen was permitted to take no other clothes than her night-dress, nor any linen. She passed Leith which was filled with soldiers ready to put down any insurrection among the people. Lords Lindsay and Ruthven took charge of her to Lochleven. Many persons imagined that the Hamiltons, and the Earl of Rothes had got together some forces for her rescue, and so Her Majesty was informed by the way, and advised therefore to linger on the road as long as possible. But this was not permitted her, for some one was always near her, who whipped her hackney to urge it on. At the edge of the Lake she was met by the Laird and his brothers, who conducted her into a room on the ground floor, furnished only with the Laird's furniture. The Queen's bed was not there, nor was there any other articles proper for one of her rank. In this prison, and in the midst of such desolation Her Majesty remained for fifteen days and more without eating, drinking, or conversing with the inmates of the house, so that many thought she would have died. . . . .

SIGNATURE OF ABDICATION.

On the afternoon of the   day of   1567, the Lords Lindsay and Ruthven, accompanied by two notaries and the said Melvil, came into the Queen's chamber. She was lying on her bed in a state of very great weakness, partly by reason of her extreme trouble (partly in consequence of a great flux, the result of a miscarriage of twins—her issue by Bothwell), so that she could move only with great difficulty. With extreme audacity and anger Lindsay gave her to understand of the commission with which he was charged by the nobility, namely, to make her sign certain letters for the resignation of the crown; which he required her to be pleased to read. Although she had already been assured by Melvil, in the name of the nobles mentioned above, that she need make no difficulty, she plainly refused to do so; she could not in conscience (her heart telling her she was innocent) prejudice her

honour by sanctioning such an unjust statement. . . . Lindsay, as soon as he
saw that Her Majesty resolutely refused to sign these letters, told her to rise from
bed, and that he had charge to carry her to a place where he could give a good
account of her to the Lords of the country. Several times he advised her to sign,
for if she did not she would compel them to cut her throat, however unwilling they
might be.

This poor princess, seeing herself thus treated by her own subjects, and being
without any of her domestics (for the two *femmes-de-chambre*, whom only she had with
her, had been turned out), . . . was compelled, by threats and present violence,
to sign these instruments, which they caused to be read by the said notaries. . . .
She protested, therefore, that she would observe and keep them no longer than
during her imprisonment, and frequently asked those who were present to be her
witnesses.

The Queen's steady firmness of purpose angered Lindsay exceedingly. He
replied (very rudely) that . . . the efficacy of these instruments did not depend
on herself, and they would take good care that she should never have the power to
revoke them. . . .

REMOVAL TO THE SQUARE TOWER.

After the Queen had signed these said letters, contrary to the promises made
to her she was taken (with great altercation on both sides) into a great gloomy
tower in Lochleven. She was there shut up within an iron gate, in such a
miserable condition that no poor criminal could be treated worse. They deprived
her of all her ink, paper, and books, and all her attendants save her two *femmes-de-
chambre* and one cook. Her surgeon was left her because she was ill, who
afterwards was of great service to her. . . . .

EXPULSION OF GEORGE DOUGLAS.

This George Douglas having had some communication with Moray about the
Queen's business, was permitted by the Earl to carry his answer back to Her
Majesty. But Moray immediately dispatched one of his own servants to Lochleven forbidding the Laird to receive his brother into his house. George having
discovered this secret message got the start of the Earl's messenger, and, having
reached Lochleven, bade Her Majesty a last farewell, after having made her
acquainted with the means she must employ in order to carry out the plan which
he had formed for her escape. She must especially endeavour to win and gain over
the person who had charge of the boats upon the lake, who was also of the same
name as the Laird. This individual was of greater importance than any of the
others for the execution of the design, for by means of him the Queen could always
learn what he (Douglas) and the other Lords of her side were doing on her behalf.
The chief of these was Lord Seton. He and the other noblemen of her party agreed
out of respect to the Queen, to forget whatever private feuds they might have among
themselves. George swore that he would faithfully render her all the loyalty and
fidelity of a good subject, protesting that he would continue to be such until death.
He carried a short letter to Lord Seton, which the Queen had written with her own
hand, though she was so closely watched that she was compelled to make her ink

with the coal which was in the chimney, for neither paper nor ink were allowed to her.

As George was leaving the Queen, his brother the Laird met him, and having told him of the prohibition which Moray had sent by his servant, commanded him at the same time to take his departure, and never again to enter the house or come near it. George was much offended therewith, and told his brother more than once that sooner or later he would be revenged, and that for the future he had better keep clear of him. Their mother was in great trouble about all this, for she was very fond of George, but on the other hand she dreaded the ruin of her elder son, and of the house.

Shortly after this occurrence George made as if he would cross near Lochleven alone, and had gone into the loch as far as his horse would carry him, in order to make a certain signal to the Queen. Hereupon his brother ordered a cannon shot to be fired at him, which was done promptly. . . . .

EXPULSION OF WILLIE DOUGLAS.

William Douglas, too, became much suspected at last; partly because when he gambled—to which he was much addicted—he made show of a large number of pieces of gold which the Queen had given him; partly because once, as he was delivering a number of letters to the Queen, which had been badly packed up, they fell to the ground in the sight of a daughter and a niece of the Laird, who generally slept with the Queen, and were always in her company. . . . .

Besides, one of these young girls having noticed William Douglas speak to the Queen, she mentioned this circumstance to the Laird. Being questioned about it William immediately admitted, through fear, that he had been solicited to carry off Her Majesty; but as he did not know the time nor the means, he could disclose nothing but in general terms, and thereupon he was expelled.

Matters, however, could not be kept so secret but that some hint of them reached the Laird's ears. Hereupon he drove William Douglas from his house, and wrote also to his brother George forbidding him henceforth, as he valued his life, to come near either the Castle or the Village on the shore of the loch. Taking advantage of this George now pretended that he had resolved to go to France, and he came to the said village for two reasons; one was to let his mother and brother know of this decision of his, the other was to ask the Queen to give him letters of recommendation and some assistance. Both the Laird and his mother were much annoyed at this resolution, for they did not wish to lose George entirely. They advised him to go to live with Moray, but this he absolutely refused to do. Hereupon the lady of Lochleven asked the Queen to write a letter commanding George to obey them in this matter, which letter she offered to send. The Queen did so, and added several particulars of news expressed in covert terms, urging him especially to hasten on the business before his sister-in-law should be astir again. George Douglas sent an answer, and then worked so successfully that, by the intercession of one of his sisters, William Douglas was recalled into the house on the last day of April. As soon as he was reinstated in his former charge, he began to make every preparation for the day which had been fixed, namely the 2nd of May. . . . .

THE QUEEN'S ESCAPE.

According to their first plan it was intended that the Queen should leap from a wall which was in the garden, of seven or eight feet in height, but she was afraid to incur the risk. Three or four days before-hand she and her two *femmes-de-chambre* pretended, as if in play, to chase each other, all going wherever the first had gone, and in this way they came to a wall in another quarter of the house equal in height to that which had to be passed. Here one of her attendants (who already had leapt), when the Queen was on the top of the wall to leap after her, became afraid of being hurt, but yet compelled herself to leap, for she thought it a matter of duty and leapt accordingly. Although she was caught when half over by one of the gentlemen of the household, yet she seriously injured one of the joints of her foot which was very weak. The Queen fearing what might happen to herself if she leapt this wall (which had to be done), namely, that she might injure herself so seriously that she would be unable to escape from the Castle, gave notice to those of her party who were to be in waiting for her on the other side of the loch, to the effect that if she should happen thus suddenly to injure herself, in that case one of her women who would remain in her chamber would let them know by a signal of fire in order that they should withdraw. This was intended more particularly for George and Lord Seton, who had a vessel ready in which they might embark and find safety in France.

When William Douglas saw how much the Queen feared this plan of leaping from the wall, he set himself about finding some other way, at once easier and less dangerous; and he proposed that she should go out by the great gate of the gate tower. With this view (having received money for the purpose) he invited the entire household to partake of a *déjeûner* on the 2nd of May, to be given in that part of the house which was farthest from that gate. The Queen and the Laird both attended, in the presence of whom, and of the whole company, William presented a branch to Her Majesty and to each person of the party calling himself "The Abbot of Unreason." He made the Queen swear and promise that for the remainder of the day she would follow him wherever he went, and then having puzzled Her Majesty, every one laughed at him as if he were drunk or a very simpleton.

The Queen remained in this part of the house during the rest of the day, as well to detain the Laird and his wife there, as to avoid the suspicion which they might have had if she had retired.

In the afternoon she threw herself upon a bed, letting it be known that she wished to rest; of which however at that time she had no great desire, although she had not slept during the whole of the previous night. While she was lying on the bed the Laird's wife was close at hand chatting with a woman who kept an Inn in the village, and who was telling her how on that very day a great troop of men on horseback had passed through the said village. Lord Seton was among them. They said they were going to an Assize, which, in the language of that county, they call a Law Day, to accompany James Hamilton of Ormiston. Also that George Douglas her brother-in-law was staying in the village, who was reputed to have come to take leave of his mother before going into France. And of a truth the Lady of Lochleven had been to visit her son, and had persuaded him, instead of going to France, to return openly to the Earl of Moray. She had given him a sum of money, and in order to confirm him in this resolution she had brought him letters from the Queen, which expressly commanded him to go to Glasgow with the greatest expedition, this being the road agreed upon between them.

Not only was the Laird's wife astir that day, but the two soldiers who had been wounded had now recovered also. One Draysdel also who served within the house as a second spy, came back on the same day from Edinburgh, where he had been expressly sent by the Queen to receive a certain sum of money of which she had made him a gift. Before he set out she had asked him to buy for her a piece of lawn with a pattern of which she had provided him, and on this pattern she had written to her officers requesting them to detain Draysdel as long as possible. And this they did very successfully.

I must not forget two very remarkable circumstances. The Laird's mother began to talk with the Queen about the report of her escape which was rife. She assured Her Majesty that such an event would be the ruin of her and her family, whereas, in time, some good understanding might be brought about between Her Majesty and Lord Moray, for the security of all. The Queen answered frankly that, since she was detained there against her will and unjustly, she would do her best, by every means in her power, to escape from prison. Yet the more freely she spoke about it the less did they trust what she said, for they supposed that if there were any truth in it she would have kept her own counsel.

The second incident was this, when this lady was walking in the garden with the Queen she saw a great troop of men on horseback riding along the opposite side of the loch, about whom she raised an outcry, and said that she would send off a messenger to ascertain who they were. To divert her from this intention Her Majesty pretended to be very angry with the Earl of Moray, so that by passing from one subject to another she kept the lady in conversation until supper time, which was intentionally delayed until everything should be ready.

Shortly after the Laird had conducted the Queen into her own room, as he was looking from the window he noticed that William Douglas was putting little pegs of wood into the chains and fixings by which the boats were fastened, one boat being excepted. This he did to prevent the Queen from being followed. Seeing this the Laird spoke roughly to William and called him a fool. The Queen became alarmed as to what might follow, and pretending that she felt very unwell, she asked for some wine. No other person being in the room, the Laird himself had to bring it, and in so doing forgot what he had seen. And again, when he was at supper, he ordered the window to be shut, which, according to custom, was left open, in order that from time to time he might look out upon the loch and notice what might be coming from the village.

As George Douglas was taking leave of his mother, he sent to the Queen, by a maid of the household who had accompanied his mother, a pearl in the shape of a pear, which Her Majesty was in the habit of wearing in one of her ears. This was understood as a signal that all was ready. Along with it he sent a message to the effect that a boatman who had found the pearl wished to sell it to him; but that he, having recognised it as her property, had sent it to her. At the same time he promised the Queen that, without fail, he would set out for Glasgow that very evening, and would never return.

An hour before supper-time the Queen retired into her own chamber. She put on a red Kirtle belonging to one of her women, and over it she covered herself with one of her own mantles. Then she went into the garden to talk with the old lady, whence she could see the people who were walking on the other side of the loch.

Everything being now ready, the Queen, who of set purpose had caused the supper to be delayed until that time, now ordered it to be served. When the supper was finished the Laird (whose ordinary custom it was to wait upon her at table) went to sup along with his wife and the rest of his household in a hall on the ground storey. A person called Draisdel, who had the chief charge in the establishment, and who generally remained in the Queen's room to keep her safe, went out along with the Laird and amused himself by playing at hand ball.

In order to free herself from the two young girls who remained with her, Her Majesty in the meantime went into an upper room above her own, occupied by her surgeon, on the plea that she wished to say her prayers; and indeed she did pray very devoutly. In this room she left her mantle, and having put on a hood such as is worn by the countrywomen of the district, she made one of her domestics who was to accompany her, dress herself in the same fashion. The other *femme-de-chambre* remained with the two young girls to amuse them for they had become very inquisitive as to the cause of the Queen's lengthened absence.

While the Laird was at supper, William Douglas, as he was handing him his drink, secretly removed the key of the great gate which lay on the table before him. He promptly gave notice of this to the Queen in order that she should come downstairs instantaneously, and immediately afterwards, as he came out of the door, he gave the sign to the young woman who was to accompany Her Majesty, as she was looking towards the window. This being understood, the Queen came down forthwith; but, as she was at the bottom of the steps, she noticed that several of the servants of the household were passing backwards and forwards in the court, which induced her to stand for some time near the door of the stairs. At last, however, in the sight of the whole of them she crossed the courtyard, and, having gone out by the great gate, William Douglas locked it with the key, and threw it into a cannon planted near at hand. The Queen and her *femme-de-chambre* had stood for some time close to the wall, fearing that they would be seen from the windows of the house; but at length they got into the vessel, and the Queen laid herself down under the boatman's seat. She had been advised to do this partly to escape notice, partly to escape being hit if a cannon shot should be sent after her. Several washerwomen and other domestics were amusing themselves in a garden near the loch, when Her Majesty got into the boat. One of the washerwomen even recognised her, and made a sign to William Douglas that she was aware of it, but William called out to her aloud by name, telling her to hold her tongue.

As the boat was nearing the other side William saw one of George's servants, but failed to recognise him as he was armed. Apprehending some fraud, he hesitated to come nearer the shore; at length, however, the servant having spoken, he landed, and then Her Majesty was met and welcomed by George Douglas and John Beton, who had broken into the Laird's stables and seized his best horses.

Being mounted as best she might, the Queen would not set off until she had seen William Douglas on horseback also—he who had hazarded so much for her release. She left her *femme-de-chambre* behind her, but with directions that she should follow her as soon as she could have an outfit.

Two miles off she met Lord Seton and the Laird of Riccarton with their followers, accompanied by whom she crossed an arm of the sea called Queensferry, where every arrangement for the purpose had been made by Lord Seton. . . . .

When the whole of the inhabitants of the village of Lochleven saw the Queen ride past, they all blessed her and prayed for her safety. No one attempted to raise any hindrance, even the Laird's uncle, who recognised her. A countryman promptly got into the boat by which the Queen had crossed, and rowed back to Lochleven Castle, to let them know by the same means that she had escaped, but the discovery had already been made by the report of the girls already mentioned, who were left in the Queen's chamber. Having gone up into the room above, and there finding her mantle, after having searched for her, they imagined that she had hidden herself for some purpose; so, not finding her, went downstairs to tell the Laird. But first they met Drysdel, of whom I have spoken above, and they told him that they could not find the Queen, and that they supposed she had escaped. Drysdel was amused at this, and said he would soon find her; he would give her leave to escape if she could. At one moment he whistled, at another he cut capers. But in the midst of these scoffs arrived the countryman with the boat, who battered at the gate, and cried out that he had seen the Queen pass through the village.

When the Laird was told of this, he fell into such a transport of frenzy that he drew his dagger to stab himself, but was prevented by the attendants. . . . .

II. Extract from "An (anonymous) Historical Account of the Deliverance of the Queen of Scotland from Captivity, 1568." *Translated by the Rev. Joseph Stevenson, S.J., from the Contemporary Latin Manuscript preserved in the Vatican at Rome.*

THE QUEEN'S ESCAPE.

WHEN the Queen knew that she could depend upon the boy she made her friends acquainted with the fact, and directed them to be in the neighbourhood on the 2nd of May, accompanied by such a number of horsemen as in their opinion might be necessary. She resolved that upon that day she would hazard the attempt when the keeper of the Castle was at supper.

There were two ways of escape from the Castle. One was by getting possession of the key of the greater gate; the other was through a certain little window, which was about the height of two cubits from the ground. It was decided that it would be better to try the gate in the first instance; for the second plan was attended by this difficulty, namely, that if the Queen in leaping from such a height should injure a limb so as to be unable to walk any further, then the whole design would be an utter failure. . . . .

In the Castle the Queen, according to her custom, supped about six o'clock. Supper being ended she went into her bed-chamber, as her keeper thought for the purpose of praying (for this was her daily custom immediately after dinner and supper), where she really meant to wait until the Laird of the Castle should sit down at table along with the warders and his own family. The Queen then put off the dress which she generally wore in the Castle, and put on that of one of her maids. The boy had placed two oars by the little window of which mention has already been made, and by their aid the Queen could easily have slid down to the ground. But not satisfied with this, and anxious to provide for every possible emergency, he determined to steal the Laird's key; and this he did with such skill that although the Laird was generally most watchful and marvellously on the alert he saw nothing of what was going on. It was the Laird's custom to place the key on the table before him while he was at supper. According to his wont the boy brought in a dish from the kitchen. Placing it on the table with one hand with the other, which was hidden by the dish, he contrived to secrete the key, leaving the dish in its place. He then hurried off to the gate with all speed. He was noticed by the maid-servant who was to accompany the Queen, who was upon the watch, and she in turn informed Her Majesty. The Queen, attended by the maid, followed the boy to the gate, going along a passage not far from the spot where the Laird was at supper. They were noticed by some of the domestics of the household, but as the Queen had changed her dress they suspected nothing amiss.

Having now reached the gate, they opened it with the least possible noise, and having gained the outside, they carefully locked it with the key, which the boy then placed inside the mouth of a cannon which happened to be lying in the court-yard. When they had got into the boat he pulled away lustily at the oars, and, having made some little way from the island the Queen held up a kerchief in her hand, thereby giving the token to those who were awaiting her on the mainland, as had been agreed upon beforehand. Having done this, she and her attendant laid themselves down on the bottom of the boat so as to be entirely out of sight, no object being visible on board save the boy at the oars. This she did in order to be safe from such shots as might be fired from the cannon or muskets in the Castle.

Beton in the meantime complained of headache, and getting up from table in the middle of supper, said that he would take a walk along the margin of the loch. Douglas followed him as he said out of kindness. They had scarcely gone a few steps when they noticed the boat pushing off from the island, and presently they observed the Queen's signal. Seton too, saw all this from the hill, and, mounting his horse dashed down to the shore as fast as it would carry him.

Although they who had been left in the village in charge of the horses had noticed the signal, yet there was some delay on their part in getting them ready. Nor could Seton come from the distant spot at which he was posted with the speed that was desired. But Beton and his companion broke open the doors of a stable situated near the shore of the loch, and saddled one of the horses which they found in it with a side saddle which was kept there. Having placed the Queen on horseback they went on the road to meet Seton. . . . .

III. ACCOUNT OF THE QUEEN'S ESCAPE GIVEN BY PETRUCCI, AMBASSADOR OF THE GRAND DUKE COSMO DE MEDICI AT THE COURT OF FRANCE, IN AN ITALIAN LETTER NOW IN THE ARCHIVES OF THE HOUSE OF MEDICI, DATED 21ST MAY 1568, AND HEADED *"modo che la Regnia de Scotia ha usata per liberam della Prigione."* *Translated from a copy of the original in Tytler's " History of Scotland,"* Vol. VII., App. vii.

THE QUEEN'S ESCAPE

" HAVING communicated with the Queen of Scots, by means of a servant of the house, Lord Seton, a most trusty catholic and right valiant gentleman, went on the day appointed with fifty cavaliers to the neighbourhood of Lochleven, where the Queen was kept captive; remaining with forty of them in the mountain near the Lake (in order not to be discovered by those in the Castle), the other ten entering a village on its bank, and pretending to be there by chance, while one of them advanced to the shore, and lying down so as not to be seen, waited till the Queen should appear, according to arrangement. At the gate of the Castle there were guards day and night, who took care that the said gate should be kept locked with a key, which was placed on the table at which the Castellan took his meals, and before his eyes. This Castellan was the uterine brother of the Earl of Moray, Regent of Scotland, natural brother of the Queen, and her mortal enemy. The Queen, after having tried to escape by a window but without success, so contrived that a page of the Castellan disposed for that office, when carrying on the 2nd of May, a dish to his master covered with a napkin, dropt the said napkin over the key, which he thus took up and carried away without any one observing. He then immediately told the Queen, who, quickly donning the dress of the taller of her two attendants left ready for the purpose, and taking the hand of the lesser, a little girl of ten years, she accompanied the page directly to the gate, opened it and went out with him and the girl, locking it outside so that no one could open it from within. She then entered a little boat kept for the service of the Castle, waving her white veil fringed with red, and thus giving the concerted signal to those who awaited her, upon which he who had been lying on the shore started up, and by another signal informed the cavaliers in the village (among whom was he who has come hither to give an account of these things to His Majesty, and who is brother to the Scotch Ambassador here). They who were in the mountain being also quickly informed immediately arrived at the lake, and the Queen, who had rowed to the shore with the page as well as she could, had arrived there by the grace of God, mounted with infinite joy on horseback with the page and the girl, and galloped to the sea coast five miles off, as by remaining on land she would have run manifest danger. Having all embarked together they conducted her to Niddry, belonging to Lord Seton, and thence to Hamilton, a castle belonging to the Duke of Chatelherault, where the Archbishop of St Andrews, his brother, and the other chiefs of her party, welcomed and acclaimed her as Queen. Hamilton is a strongly fortified place about five leagues from Dumbarton, which is a very strong Castle; but the Queen did not retire there, feeling safe at Hamilton, which commands all that county.

The whole kingdom is in commotion, some for the Queen, some against her, and with the Earl of Moray. She has sent this gentleman (John Beaton) to ask a thousand musketeers of His Majesty; but for the recovery of Edinburgh and other fortresses occupied by the rebels, she will have need of all further help, and has written a letter to the Cardinal of Lorraine which would move the hardest heart to compassion for her, in the first lines of which she asks pardon of God and the world for the past errors of her youth, acknowledging her liberation is due to the Divine Majesty alone, and giving humble thanks that so much courage has been granted to her in her afflictions, expressing her firm determination to live and die a catholic now more than ever."

Edinburgh: George Waterston & Sons, Printers.

CPSIA information can be obtained at www.ICGtesting.com
Printed in the USA
LVOW09s1316150515

438675LV00015B/175/P

9 781297 290930